JACOB MAXWELL

TRIVIA FOR SENIORS:
MUSIC AND MOVIES

OUR READER'S
FAVORITE TRIVIA CORNER

After attacking Pearl Harbor on Dec
7th 1942, what famous quote did
General Isoroku Yamamoto give?

*"I fear we have awakened
a leeping giant and filled him with
an awesome resolve."*

HARRY J. FEICK

BOOST YOUR MEMORY FOR FREE!

Stay young in mind and young at heart with bonus rounds.

Join our TRIVIA TRIBE NOW!

HAVE YOUR NAME IN THE CREDITS

Send us your favorite trivia question for a chance to have it included in our next trivia book. And yes, we'll have you in the credits!

Simply send us an email to:
funtriviawithjacob@gmail.com

DOWNLOAD OUR BOOKS FOR FREE!

You're one click away from our best-selling books. Scan the QR code or follow the link below to download all our trivia books for FREE. Take advantage of this limited opportunity.

https://bit.ly/FunTriviaCollection

TABLE OF CONTENTS

I think I'm a trivia nerd.

I love to learn about everything.

I'm curious.

Adam Rodriguez

INTRODUCTION

There's nothing more exciting than re-living magical moments than through music and movies that captured our hearts!

This is why we've prepared quite the Trivia memory game for you. **Trivia for Seniors: Music and Movies Edition** is here to improve your long-term memory, working memory, and processing speed as you have the fun of your life blasting old tunes and practicing classical movie lines.

What are you waiting for? Turn to the next page and rediscover your favorite music, and put your movie knowledge to the test!

THE MUSICIANS

OF THE 1940S

THE MUSICIANS OF THE 1940S

1. She sang "God Bless The Child" and "Summertime." Who was this great lady who sang the Blues?
   a. Billie Holiday
   b. Sarah Vaughan
   c. Nina Simone
   d. Ella Fitzgerald

2. Who was this famous crooner who began his career in the 1940s, and was always linked to Italian organized crime?
   a. Tony Bennett
   b. Bing Crosby
   c. Frank Sinatra
   d. Perry Como

3. Of what type of musical group was Count Basie the leader?
   a. Quintet
   b. Orchestra
   c. Trio
   d. Quartet

4. Which memorable singer of the 1940s had the song, "Unforgettable," as his signature song?
   a. Cab Calloway
   b. Slim Gaillard
   c. Fats Waller
   d. Nat King Cole

5. Ella Fitzgerald was known as "Lady Ella" and the "First Lady of Song." Of what type of music was she known as the Queen?
   a. Jazz
   b. Swing
   c. Bebop
   d. Country

6. If you're listening to an old version of "White Christmas," then chances are, you are listening

to this singer who became famous in the 1940s. Who was he?

    a. Buddy Clark

    b. Dick Powell

    c. Bing Crosby

    d. Jerry Wayne

7. Dinah Shore is famous for being one of the earlier interpreters of this now controversial Christmas song. What was the name of the song?

    a. Santa Baby

    b. Baby, it's Cold Outside

    c. Jingle Bells

    d. Winter Wonderland

8. Louis Armstrong may be known for his gravelly singing voice, but what was his musical instrument?

    a. Saxophone

    b. Drums

    c. Piano

    d. Trumpet

9. What was the name of this George Gershwin song about infatuation, sung by Sarah Vaughan?
    a. The Man I love
    b. Embraceable You
    c. I've Got a Crush on You
    d. Someone to Watch Over Me

10. One of Glenn Miller's most famous songs was about getting you into this. What was the song?
    a. Kalamazoo
    b. In the Mood
    c. Moonlight Serenade
    d. Fools Rush In

11. Were the Andrews Sisters really sisters?
    a. Yes
    b. No
    c. Some were
    d. Only by marriage

12. This 1946 song from crooner Perry Como describes him as a prisoner of this. What is "this?"
    a. Hate
    b. Destiny
    c. Desire
    d. Love

13. What was patriotic singer Jo Stafford known as when she was an entertainer for the troops?
    a. Sergeant Stafford
    b. G.I. Jo
    c. Ms. Iron Lungs
    d. Miss American Jo

14. Cab Calloway was singing about a girl hooked on drugs in this famous early song of his. What was the song?
    a. Junker's Blues

b. Who put the Benzedrine in Mrs. Murphy's Ovaltine?

c. Minnie the Moocher

d. The Reefer Song

15. Eartha Kitt was a talented singer who could sing in more than one language. What was the other language that she used in many of her songs?

    a. French

    b. Arabic

    c. Chinese

    d. Swahili

16. What song did patriotic composer Irving Berlin write, which became practically a national anthem during World War II?

    a. Let's Go West Again

    b. God Bless America

    c. How About a Cheer for the Navy

    d. American Eagles

17. "Anything Goes" for this talented composer, who is "Easy to Love" if you're willing to "Experiment." Who was this talented guy?

a. Cole Porter
b. Tex Ritter
c. Roy Milton
d. George Formby

18. In 1944, Jimmy Dorsey's orchestra backed Kitty Kallen for this famous Mexican song about being too passionate. What song was this?
    a. La Cucaracha
    b. Perfidia
    c. El Rancho Grande
    d. Besame Mucho

19. What was 1940s' bebop pioneer Charlie Parker's preferred musical instrument?
    a. Saxophone
    b. Flute
    c. Trombone
    d. Piano

20. In the '40s, Frank Sinatra briefly became a featured vocalist of a popular orchestra led by this man. Who was this bandleader?
    a. Johnny Mathis
    b. Buddy Clark

c. Harry James

d. Dean Martin

21. Benny Goodman was known as the King. But what was he the King of?

    a. Jazz

    b. Ballroom

    c. Pop

    d. Swing

22. Sammy Kaye's signature song was about a special set of lights. What were these lights?

    a. Christmas lights

    b. Harbor lights

    c. Runway lights

    d. Highway lights

23. Dizzy Gillespie helped develop this style of jazz. What was it called?
    a. Calypso
    b. Bebop
    c. Afro-Cuban
    d. Progressive

24. There were many saxophonists who were bandleaders, but for what kind of saxophone was Freddy Martin known?
    a. Soprano saxophone
    b. Alto saxophone
    c. Baritone sax
    d. Tenor sax

25. The Mills Brothers had a big hit in the 1940s with "Paper Doll." What was the song about?
    a. A girl thinking of her wedding day
    b. A man jilted by his girlfriend for another
    c. It's literally about paper dolls.
    d. True love

26. Vaughn Monroe was the first to record this ode to winter weather and Christmas. What was that song?

a. Deck The Halls
b. Santa Baby
c. Let it Snow, Let it Snow, Let it Snow
d. Jingle Bells

27. "Take the A Train" became the signature theme of Duke Ellington's orchestra in the 1940s. Where was the train going?
    a. New Orleans
    b. Detroit
    c. Chicago
    d. Harlem

28. Tommy Dorsey was known for the great people in his band, but how did he get all these talented people?
    a. He got them from other big bands.
    b. He trained them.
    c. He looked at amateur performers.
    d. He put ads out in the papers.

29. Hank Williams was a big star again by the end of the 1940s, but what problem stalled his career in the beginning?
    a. Divorce

b. Alcoholism

c. Nervous breakdown

d. Family tragedy

30. Roy Rogers was another man who was known as the King in the 1940s. What was he the King of?

    a. Ballads

    b. Dance

    c. Country

    d. Jazz

31. He got "Georgia on My Mind" during "The Right Time," yeah, "What'd I Say?" Who was this musical prodigy?

a. Willie Johnson
b. Stevie Wonder
c. George Shearing
d. Ray Charles

32. Gene Autry was so popular that he had rules that reflected his do-good personality. What was the name of these rules?
    a. The Ten Commandments
    b. The Cowboy Code
    c. The Gentleman's Rules
    d. Good manners and Right Conduct

33. Multi-talented Eddie Cantor was a versatile musician, but his greatest musical creation is a TV theme song. What kind of TV show was it?
    a. A soap opera show
    b. A Western show
    c. A cartoon show
    d. A late-night talk show

34. What made the Ink Spots unusual in some of the places where they played?
    a. They were African-American
    b. They were very tall

c. They had no orchestra

d. They were not patriotic

35. Who was Dean Martin's performance partner in the 1940s?
    a. Tony Bennett
    b. Sammy Davis Jr.
    c. Frank Sinatra
    d. Jerry Lewis

ANSWER KEY

THE MUSICIANS OF THE 1940S

1.	A	22.	B
2.	C	23.	C
3.	B	24.	D
4.	D	25.	B
5.	A	26.	C
6.	C	27.	D
7.	B	28.	A
8.	D	29.	B
9.	C	30.	C
10.	B	31.	D
11.	A	32.	B
12.	D	33.	C
13.	B	34.	A
14.	C	35.	D
15.	A		
16.	B		
17.	A		
18.	D		
19.	A		
20.	C		
21.	D		

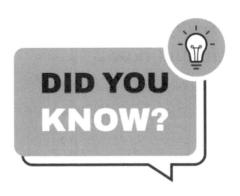

DID YOU KNOW?

Music from the 1940s reflected a wide spectrum of tastes, ranging from swing band numbers like "In the Mood," "Tuxedo Junction" and "Take the 'A' Train," to strictly Tin Pan Alley tunes like "Paper Doll" and "Buttons and Bows."

Here's a brief list of tunes that were a million sellers in the decade.

- "In the Mood"
- "Tuxedo Junction"
- "Rum and Coca-Cola"
- "Sentimental Journey"
- "White Christmas"
- "Take the 'A' Train"
- "God Bless the Child"
- "Chattanooga Choo Choo"
- "You Made Me Love You"
- "Paper Doll"

- "You Always Hurt the One You Love"
- "Buttons and Bows"
- "On a Slow Boat to China"

In general, tunes that became jazz standards from the 1940s tended to be from Tin Pan Alley, with Broadway show tunes being replaced by tunes from movies (for example, "Chattanooga Choo Choo"). There was a higher proportion of numbers written and performed by jazz artists like "Night in Tunisia," "Perdido," "Good Bait" and "Four Brothers."

THE BEST OF 1950S

THE BEST OF 1950S

1. Name the artist who made history by becoming the first African-American woman to win a Grammy Award.
   a. Ella Fitzgerald
   b. Etta James
   c. Tina Turner
   d. Billie Holiday

2. Which artist recorded the song "Your Cheatin' Heart".
   a. Johnny Otis
   b. Jimmy Reed
   c. Hank Williams
   d. Bill Monroe

3. Name The Beatles' album that sold the most copies in Britain.
   a. "Help!"
   b. "Let It Be"
   c. "Abbey Road"
   d. "Sgt. Peppers Lonely Hearts Club Band"

4. Which singer is known for songs like "Crazy He Calls Me" and "Strange Fruit".
   a. Billie Holiday
   b. B.B. King
   c. Loretta Lynn
   d. Ike Turner

5. "Godfather of Rhythm and Blues" is the title of?
   a. Tony Bennett
   b. Johnny Otis
   c. Elvis Presley
   d. Paul Anka

6. Which singer has the nickname of "King of Swing"?
   a. Tony Bennett
   b. Perry Como
   c. Benny Goodman
   d. Chuck Berry

7. What was the name of the music group that Bill Monroe formed?
   a. The Backroad Group
   b. The Blue Grass Boys
   c. The Pioneers
   d. The Beatles

8. Name the musician who was responsible for helping to create who we know as Tina Turner.
    a. Ike Turner
    b. B.B. King
    c. James Brown
    d. Tennessee Ernie Ford

9. Which musician hosted a musical television show in the late '50s?
    a. Billie Holiday
    b. Loretta Lynn
    c. Perry Como
    d. Jimmy Reed

10. Who sang "The Wallflower"?
    a. Etta James
    b. Brenda Lee

c. Bing Crosby

d. Johnny Horton

11. Which artist created a song so iconic that it became an official state song?
    a. Nat King Cole
    b. Paul Anka
    c. Glen Campbell
    d. Ray Charles

12. Which song by Nat King Cole was later made into a duet by his daughter?
    a. "Unforgettable"
    b. "To the Ends of the Earth"
    c. "Star dust"
    d. "Mona Lisa"

13. Which artist recorded the song "Everybody Loves Somebody"?
    a. The Beatles
    b. Elvis Presley
    c. Etta James
    d. Dean Martin

14. Name the group that made music solely with their voices.
    a. The Mills Brothers
    b. The Beatles
    c. God Bless America
    d. The Oak Ridge Boys

15. "Rhinestone Cowboy" was _____.
    a. Johnny Cash
    b. Glen Campbell
    c. Bing Crosby
    d. Jimmy Reed

16. Johnny Cash did not write which song?
    a. "Get Rhythm"
    b. "This Town"
    c. "Ring of Fire"
    d. "I Walk the Line"

17. Name the hit Patsy Cline song earned her three standing ovations at the Grand Ole Opry.
    a. "Heartaches"
    b. "I Fall to Pieces"
    c. "Crazy"
    d. "Walkin' After Midnight"

18. Which was Buddy Holly's only number one song?
    a. "That'll Be the Day"
    b. "Peggy Sue"
    c. "Baby I Don't Care"
    d. "Raining in my Heart"

19. Which song became an accidental hit for Tennessee Ernie Ford?
    a. "Riding A Raid"
    b. "Mule Train"
    c. "Sixteen Tons"
    d. "I'll Never Be Free"

20. Who wrote the theme song for the "Tonight Show with Johnny Carson"?
    a. Tony Bennett
    b. Paul Anka

c. Buddy Holly

d. Fats Domino

21. Name the artist who is said to have created the first song in the Rock N' Roll genre.
   a. Perry Como
   b. Fats Domino
   c. Carl Perkins
   d. Miles Davis

22. The historical song "The Battle of New Orleans" was sung by?
   a. Etta James
   b. Johnny Horton
   c. Tony Bennett
   d. Ike Turner

23. Which artist had incredible guitar skills?
   a. B.B. King
   b. Miles Davis
   c. Ella Fitzpatrick
   d. Bing Crosby

24. "Rockin' Around the Clock" was sung by
_____.
   a. Brenda Lee
   b. Patsy Cline
   c. Tina Turner
   d. Etta James

25. Which song was on the "A" side of Roy Orbison's track "Yo te Amo Maria".
   a. "Born on the Wind"
   b. "It's Over"
   c. "Oh, Pretty Woman"
   d. "You Got It"

26. Recorded in 1952, "Auf Wiederseh'n Sweetheart" was a US Number 1 hit for which singer?
   a. Vera Lynn
   b. Rosemary Clooney
   c. Patti Page
   d. Kay Starr

27. "I Can Dream, Can't I" was a Number 1 hit for 4 weeks in 1950. Name the artist.
   a. The Michaels Sisters
   b. The Davids Sisters

    c. The Daniels Sisters

    d. The Andrews Sisters

28. Carlos Wilson and Edward Bowers were members of which American doo-wop vocal group?

    a. The Dominoes

    b. The Platters

    c. The Cadillacs

    d. The Clovers

29. One of the pioneers of rock and roll music, Chuck Berry is most known for playing which instrument?

    a. Drums

    b. Trumpet

    c. Piano

    d. Guitar

30. Mercury Record's first successful female artist, Clara Ann Fowler is the real name of which of these 1950s stars?

    a. June Valli

    b. Peggy Lee

    c. Patti Page

    d. Doris Day

31. "Good Night Irene" was a 1950 Number 1 hit for Gordon Jenkins and….?
    a. The Dolls
    b. The Spinners
    c. The Weavers
    d. The Jets

32. How old was Sam Cooke when he was fatally shot by Bertha Franklin in Los Angeles, California?
    a. 55
    b. 22
    c. 33
    d. 44

33. Best known for her two number-one hits, "Wheel of Fortune" and "The Rock And Roll

Waltz," Katherine Laverne Starks was the real name of which 1950s singer?

   a. Peggy Lee

   b. Patti Page

   c. Kay Starr

   d. Rosemary Clooney

34. Only You (And You Alone)" was the debut hit for which American vocal group?

   a. The Cadillacs

   b. The Clovers

   c. The Dominoes

   d. The Platters

35. Known for his trademark dark sunglasses, "The Big O" was the nickname given to which star?

   a. Bobby Darin

   b. Huey Smith

   c. Roy Orbison

   d. Ritchie Valens

36. Tony Bennett had a 1951 Number 1 hit with the song "Cold, Cold...."?

   a. Night

   b. Heart

c. You

d. Day

37. What was Elvis Presley's last Number 1 hit song of the 1950s?

    a. Wooden Heart

    b. It's Now or Never

    c. A Big Hunk o' Love

    d. Stuck on You

38. Which of these acts was first to have a Number 1 on the US Billboard Chart in the 1950s?

    a. Gene Autry

    b. Patti Page

    c. Nat King Cole

    d. Red Foley

39. Which popular doo-wop group had hits in the 1950s with "Star Dust" and "Have Mercy Baby"?

    a. The Clovers

    b. The Cadillacs

    c. The Platters

    d. The Dominoes

40. Ranked number 69 on Rolling Stone's 100 Greatest Artists of All Time list, who was often billed as "Mr. Excitement"?
    a. Jackie Wilson
    b. Little Willie John
    c. Frankie Lymon
    d. Chuck Willis

ANSWER KEY

THE BEST OF 1950S

1. A	23. A
2. C	24. A
3. D	25. C
4. A	26. A
5. B	27. D
6. C	28. D
7. B	29. D
8. A	30. C
9. C	31. C
10. A	32. C
11. D	33. C
12. A	34. D
13. D	35. C
14. A	36. B
15. B	37. C
16. C	38. A
17. C	39. D
18. A	40. A
19. C	
20. B	
21. B	
22. B	

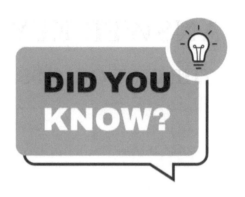

Recording Advancements

Four-track recordings began to appear with Les Paul and Mary Ford's "How High the Moon" in 1951. The record hit number one on the Billboard chart for 9 weeks and is a NARAS Hall of Fame selection.

Early 1950s

Perry Como was a leading lounge act of the early 1950s along with Dean Martin, Nat King Cole, and Frank Sinatra. Patti Page and Jo Stafford were leading female artists. Hank Williams had built up a string of Top 10 country hits at the time of his death in 1953 at the age of 39.

Early Rockers

Rock 'n' roll was a term used in R&B songs as far back as the 1930s, but was first used to describe a musical genre by Cleveland radio disc jockey Alan Freed in the early 1950s. Early rock 'n' roll songs include "Rocket 88" by Ike Turner and "Shake, Rattle & Roll" by Big Joe Turner.

Elvis, Top Artists

In 1955 "Rock Around the Clock" by Bill Haley & His Comets became the first rock 'n' roll record to top the Billboard singles chart. Elvis Presley began having national hits in 1956 starting with "Heartbreak Hotel." Other artists that popularized the new music were Chuck Berry, Little Richard, Jerry Lee Lewis, and Carl Perkins.

Buddy Holly

Buddy Holly & The Crickets had popular hit singles including "That'll Be the Day" before a fatal plane crash on Feb. 3, 1959, killed Holly, The Big Bopper, and Richie Valens, whose biggest hit was a rendition of "La Bamba."

Late 1950s

Several pop standards of the 1930s and 1940s were hits again in the late 1950s, such as Bobby Darin's "Mack the Knife" and The Platters' "Smoke Gets In Your Eyes." Doo-wop became an established sound while R&B was popularized by Ray Charles.

THE SOUNDTRACK

OF 1960S

THE SOUNDTRACK OF 1960S

1. Can you tell the name of the group that had a hit car song with "Hey Little Cobra" in 1964?
   a. The Ripchords
   b. The Astronauts
   c. Johnny and the Daytonas
   d. The Beach Boys

2. The Beatles had the top five songs for much of the beginning of 1964. Which artist or group knocked the Beatles "She Loves You" out of Number One May 1964?
   a. Frank Sinatra
   b. The Supremes
   c. The Four Seasons
   d. Louis Armstrong

3. Which singer was known for performing his hit, "FIRE" while being lowered on stage in a flaming headdress?
   a. Jimi Hendrix
   b. Arthur Brown
   c. Screamin' Jay Hawkins
   d. Alice Cooper

4. Name the group with the hit song, "Concrete and Clay".
    a. We Five
    b. Unit 4 plus Two
    c. Dave Clark Five
    d. Count Five

5. "Banana" was the lead guitarist for _____ group.
    a. The Strawberry Alarm Clock
    b. The Lovin' Spoonful
    c. The Turtles
    d. The Youngbloods

6. Cheesy "pyschodelic" were a trend in the late sixties. Name the group that had a hit with "Green Tambourine".
    a. Every Mother's Son
    b. Spiral Staircase
    c. The Lemon Pipers
    d. The Byrds

7. Who wrote the song "Dandy" that was a hit for Herman's Hermits in the US?
    a. The Kinks

b. The Yardbirds

c. The Animals

d. The Nazz

8. The song 1, 2, 3 was a hit for _____.
   a. Lou Christie
   b. Jackson Five
   c. Len Barry
   d. Frankie Valli

9. The song "Respect" that was recorded by Aretha Franklin in 1967 was originally sung by _____.
   a. Otis Redding
   b. Smokey Robinson
   c. Dionne Warwick
   d. Ray Charles

10. Which popular artist recorded 'Papa's Got a Brand New Bag' in 1965?
    a. James Brown
    b. Jackie Wilson
    c. Jimi Hendrix
    d. Carole King

11. 'Long Tall Sally' was originally recorded by _____ and its remake was recorded by The Beatles in 1964.
    a. Chuck Berry
    b. Buddy Holly
    c. Little Richard
    d. James Brown

12. The Ronettes recorded 'Be My Baby' in 1963. Name the man who produced and co-wrote it.
    a. Phil Spector
    b. Jeff Barry
    c. Hal Blaine
    d. Gerry Goffin

13. Can you name Otis Redding's only number one hit just three days before he died in a plane crash.

a. Try A Little Tenderness
b. (Sittin' On The) Dock of the Bay
c. Respect
d. Pain In My Heart

14. Name the song by lyrics: 'The way you smell so sweet, you know you could have been some perfume'.
    a. I've Been Loving You Too Long
    b. You've Really Got A Hold On Me
    c. The Way You Do The Things You Do
    d. Stop! In The Name Of Love

15. 'All Along The Watchtower' was recorded by Jimi Hendrix in 1968. _____ was the original songwriter and singer of this song.
    a. Carole King
    b. Janis Joplin
    c. Bob Dylan
    d. Ray Charles

16. Name the super talented singer-songwriter of the 60s died of a drug overdose just at the prime of her career.
    a. Carole King

b. Aretha Franklin

c. Grace Slick

d. Janis Joplin

17. Name the rock band who stayed together for thirty years till their lead singer died in 1995.

    a. The Grateful Dead

    b. The Doors

    c. The Rolling Stones

    d. Jefferson Airplane

18. _____ song gave Elvis Presley his first US No.1 of the 60's.

    a. None of the Above

    b. "It's Now or Never"

    c. "A Big Hunk o' Love"

    d. "Stuck on You"

19. _____ scored the 1961 US No.1 hit "Big Bad John".
    a. Jimmy Dean
    b. Ricky Nelson
    c. Bobby Vinton
    d. Jimi Hendrix

20. Which band scored the US No.1 hit "Rag Doll" in 1964.
    a. None of the above
    b. Gary Lewis & The Playboys
    c. The Shangri-Las
    d. The Four Seasons

21. Which British group became the first to top the US singles charts?
    a. The Animals
    b. The Tornados
    c. The Beatles
    d. The Byrds

22. Who wrote "I'm into Something Good" a No.1 hit for Herman's Hermits in 1964?
    a. Phil Spector & Barry Mann
    b. Barry Mann & Carol King

c. Graham Gouldman

d. Gerry Goffin & Carol King

23. Which singer performed the theme tune for the James Bond version Thunderball in 1966?
    a. Tom Jones
    b. Shirley Bassey
    c. Ricky Nelson
    d. Engelbert Humperdinck

24. Which band plays an important role in the careers of Jimmy Page, Jeff Beck, and Eric Clapton?
    a. The Monkees
    b. The Searchers
    c. The Kinks
    d. The Yardbirds

25. Which artist invented the music production technique called The Wall of Sound in the 1960s?
    a. Phil Everly
    b. Phil Evans
    c. Phil Spector
    d. Phil Collins

26. Peter Noone was the lead singer of which band?
    a. Herman's Hermits
    b. Manfred Man
    c. The Shangri-Las
    d. The Tremeloes

27. In the name of the American funk band Booker T.& the M.G.'s, what does M.G stand for?
    a. Miami Group
    b. Maine Group
    c. Massachusetts Group
    d. Memphis Group

28. "But now these days have gone. I'm not so self assured." These lyrics are from which song by the Beatles?
    a. "Here Come the Sun"
    b. "Hey Jude"

c. "Let It Be"

d. "Help"

29. "It's Now or Never" was the first number one of which singer in the 1960s?
    a. Elvis Presley
    b. Tom Jones
    c. Bob Dylan
    d. Brian Hyland

30. What was the best-selling single in the United Kingdom during the 60s?
    a. "I Got You Babe"
    b. "Wouldn't It Be Nice"
    c. "Tears"
    d. "She Loves You"

31. This song was the first number one of Tom Jones in 1965, which was popularized later in the Fresh Prince of Bel-Air by Carlton. What was it?
    a. "It's Not Unusual"
    b. "The Sun Died"
    c. "I'll Never Fall in Love Again"
    d. "Daughter of Darkness"

32. Which singer performed the original version of "Itsy Bitsy Teenie Weenie Yellow Polkadot Bikini," which later on became a hit by Bombalurina in 1990?
    a. Andy Williams
    b. Tom Jones
    c. David Bowie
    d. Brian Hyland

33. Here comes the last one on this list of 60s music quiz questions and answers: in 1964, which girl group had a worldwide hit with "Chapel of Love?
    a. The Dixie-Cups
    b. Martha and the Vandellas
    c. The Paris Sisters
    d. The Ronettes

34. What Janis Ian song was banned by several radio stations in 1967?
    a. Society's Child
    b. At Seventeen
    c. Roses
    d. Jesse

35. What did Jimi Hendrix first do in March of 1967?
   a. Set fire to his guitar while on stage
   b. Performed in a Broadway show
   c. Collaborated with other performers
   d. Toured Australia

ANSWER KEY

THE SOUNDTRACK OF 1960S

1. A
2. D
3. B
4. B
5. D
6. C
7. A
8. C
9. A
10. A
11. C
12. A
13. B
14. C
15. C
16. D
17. A
18. D
19. A
20. D
21. B

22. D
23. A
24. D
25. C
26. A
27. D
28. D
29. A
30. D
31. A
32. D
33. A
34. A
35. A

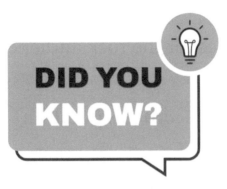

The First British Invasion

The Beatles generally get the credit for starting the British Invasion in 1964. However, two British records scored the top spot on Billboard's Top 100 in 1962. Acker Bilk's "Stranger on the Shore" and The Tornadoes' "Telstar" were both one-hit wonders in the U.S. However, orchestra leader Annunzio Paolo Mantovani was a resident of the U.K. from the age of 7. Between 1955 and 1972, more than 40 albums by his orchestra made the charts in the U.S., providing a wealth of easy-listening music for the rock audience to disdain.

The Motown Record Corporation

Based in Detroit and started by former car factory worker Berry Gordy, Motown had much in common with the assembly lines that fed car-crazy America. Songwriters such as Smoky Robinson and the team of Holland, Dozier, Holland provided the fuel for artists that included the Miracles, the Temptations and Martha and the Vandellas. Under the hood, though, were the high-horsepower Funk Brothers, a collection of studio musicians who likely played on more hits than the combined totals of the Beatles, Rolling Stones, Beach Boys and Elvis Presley.

The Festival Explosion

Communing with nature to a rock backbeat may seem to be the quintessential 1960s music experience, and with good reason. The Monterey International Pop Festival of 1967 started three years of classic outdoor rock festivals -- although Bob Dylan did play his first rock set at the 1965 Newport Folk Festival. Festivals followed in Miami, various locations under the Newport Pop label, Atlanta and Atlantic City, New Jersey. The yin and the yang of the '60s festivals were Woodstock and Altamont, in August and December 1969, respectively

The Guitars

The big four electric guitars were Telecasters and Stratocasters made by Fender, and Les Pauls and

SGs, both Gibson models. The Telecaster's design had mass production in mind, not aesthetics or tone. Those features were built into the Stratocaster in spades, and it may well be the most influential electric guitar. Les Pauls were named for the guitarist and inventor. When sales went soft, Gibson introduced the SG but called these models Les Pauls until the stock of "Les Paul" truss rod cover plates was exhausted.

THE WONDERFUL

MUSIC OF 1970S

THE WONDERFUL MUSIC OF 1970S

1. The Doors was the first band ever to advertise a new album on what?
   a. bill board
   b. yard sign
   c. newspaper
   d. radio

2. Led Zeppelin came up with the name "Black Dog" because?
   a. They loved black dogs.
   b. Lead singer, Robert Plant, had a black dog named Midnight.
   c. A black dog walked into Robert Plant's living room in the middle of the night.
   d. A black lab walked into the recording studio as they were recording the song.

3. Lynyrd Skynyrd got their name from a high school teacher, Leonard Skinner, who suspended students for what?
   a. wearing the color green
   b. chewing gum in the hallways
   c. having long hair
   d. not wearing socks

4. How many musical instruments was Brian Jones, co-founder of The Rolling Stones proficient at?
   a. 30
   b. 60
   c. 10
   d. 20

5. Queen has the longest-running _____ according to the Guinness Book of World Records.
   a. songs
   b. record spent at #1 on the Top 40 charts
   c. display held at the Rock and Roll Hall of Fame
   d. fan club

6. Malcolm Young, AC/DC guitarist, worked as a sewing-machine mechanic where?
   a. cloth factory
   b. coat factory
   c. undergarment factory
   d. shoe factory

7. John Denver's song "Take Me Home, Country Roads", is about _____ U.S. State.
   a. Tennessee
   b. California
   c. West Virginia
   d. Colorado

8. Name the blonde bombshell who became the face of country music in the early 1970s.
   a. Dolly Parton
   b. Marilyn Monroe
   c. None of the above
   d. Debra Harry

9. Name the family band was all the rage in the early 70s with their #1 hit, "I Want You Back"?
   a. The Partridge Family
   b. The Brady Bunch Band

c. The Familia

d. The Jackson 5

10. Can you complete the sentence: "You're so _____, you probably think this song is about you".
    a. desperate
    b. selfish
    c. vain
    d. curious

11. In 1970, the Kinks had an international top ten hit with "Lola." According to the song's opening lines, where did the singer meet Lola?
    a. on a beach in Hot Rio
    b. in a club in Old Soho
    c. at a pub in Kokomo
    d. at a bar in Chicago

12. In 1970, the band Free reached the top five on the Billboard charts with their rocker "All Right Now". Name the member of the band who sang lead vocals.
    a. Paul Rodgers
    b. Andy Fraser

c. Simon Kirke

d. Paul Kossoff

13. Complete the lyrics from 1970's hit "Venus": "A goddess on a mountain top was burning like a _____. The summit of beauty in love, and Venus was her name"

    a. Silver flame

    b. Roaring train

    c. Golden sun

    d. Hurricane

14. In 1970, which Detroit-born singer had a U.S. hit single with "Band of Gold"?

    a. Bobby Sherman

    b. Freda Payne

    c. Anne Murray

    d. Bobbi Martin

15. In January 1970, name the singer who struck gold with the single "Raindrops Keep Fallin' on My Head".

    a. Eddie Holman

    b. Neil Diamond

    c. Mark Lindsay

    d. B. J. Thomas

16. In 1970, John Lennon achieved success with his single "Instant Karma!". The following natural object was not mentioned in the song's chorus.
    a. The sun
    b. The stars
    c. The sea
    d. The moon

17. Complete the song "Ride Captain Ride" lyrics: "_____ men sailed up from the San Francisco Bay."
    a. seventy-three
    b. one-hundred
    c. seventy-six
    d. eighty-six

18. Can you complete the title of a top ten U.S. hit song by the Poppy Family: "Which Way You Goin' _____."
    a. Poppy
    b. Vinny
    c. Tommy
    d. Billy

19. Name the singer of 'Everything Is Beautiful'.
    a. Brian Hyland
    b. Glen Campbell
    c. Tom Jones
    d. Ray Stevens

20. According to R. Dean Taylor, name the state wanted him in his song.
    a. North Dakota
    b. Indiana
    c. Alabama
    d. California

21. Aside from English, what other language is the song 'Look What They've Done to My Song, Ma' by the New Seekers also available?
    a. Spanish

b. Japanese
c. Portuguese
d. French

22. Who sang 'Julie, Do Ya Love Me' ?
    a. Ray Stevens
    b. Bobby Sherman
    c. B.J. Thomas
    d. Tom Jones

23. Who was the singer of 'Son of a Preacher Man'?
    a. Martha and the Vandellas
    b. Dusty Springfield
    c. Gladys Knight and the Pips
    d. Supremes

24. In 'El Condor Pasa', he would rather be _____.
    a. forest
    b. snail
    c. street
    d. nail

25. On January 1 2005, the Canadian Broadcasting
    Corporation held a poll that voters could vote
    on, naming the greatest song in the century.

Virgin Radio and Nine Network conducted similar surveys (at differing dates). All three radio stations chose this one song from 1971. What was the song?

    a.   Across the Universe by The Beatles
    b.   Imagine by John Lennon
    c.   Hey Jude by The Beatles
    d.   Dancing Queen by ABBA

26. What three genres did progressive rock music incorporate?

    a.   classical, jazz, and world
    b.   punk, rock, and psychedelia
    c.   country, folk, and blues
    d.   jazz, punk, and blues

27. Which band released the song Iron Man in 1970?

    a.   Queen
    b.   Black Sabbath
    c.   AC/DC
    d.   The Bee Gees

28. Which musician got the song Lovin' You to the top of the charts in 1975?

a. Minnie Riperton
b. Ray Stevens
c. Maureen McGovern
d. Led Zeppelin

29. What was the most commercially successful album by Pink Floyd?
    a. A Nice Pair
    b. The Wall
    c. Dark Side of the Moon
    d. Meddle

30. Which song served as the Bee Gees's rebound after their failed album, Life in a Tin Can?
    a. Main Course
    b. Children of the New World
    c. Mr. Natural
    d. Stayin' Alive

31. How did folk and country musician Bob Dylan adapt to the 1970s?
    a. He moved to the rural Midwest.
    b. He switched to heavy metal.
    c. He did not do anything about it.
    d. He helped pioneer country rock.

32. In the first half of the 1970s, which of these bands were at the height of their international fame?
    a. KISS
    b. Queen
    c. Aerosmith
    d. ABBA

33. What musical genre is a prime influence in the works of The Clash?
    a. punk
    b. ska
    c. jazz
    d. disco

34. What were two early British acts who popularized the punk rock genre?

a. The Sex Pistols and The Clash
b. The Rolling Stones and The Move
c. The Beatles and The Who
d. The Clash and The Who

35. Which Doobie Brothers song hit #1 in 1979?
    a. It Keeps You Runnin'
    b. What a Fool Believes
    c. With a Little Luck
    d. Baby's Request

ANSWER KEY

THE WONDERFUL MUSIC OF 1970S

1.	A	22.	B
2.	D	23.	B
3.	C	24.	B
4.	D	25.	B
5.	D	26.	A
6.	C	27.	B
7.	C	28.	A
8.	A	29.	C
9.	D	30.	A
10.	C	31.	D
11.	B	32.	B
12.	A	33.	B
13.	A	34.	A
14.	B	35.	B
15.	D		
16.	C		
17.	A		
18.	D		
19.	D		
20.	B		
21.	D		

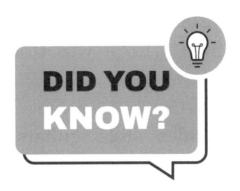

1. The title track for "Paranoid" (1970) was only written after Black Sabbath realized they didn't have enough songs for the album.

2. Queen's "A Night At The Opera" (1975) was the most expensive album ever made at the time of its release.

3. Ian Gillan contracted hepatitis just before deep purple began recording "Machine Head" (1972).

4. The Clash's debut album (1977) was recorded in a flat rented by Mick Jones' grandmother.

5. It took three hours to shoot the cover photo for Bruce Springsteen's "Born To Run" (1975).

6. The repeated, insane laughter in "Dark Side Of The Moon" (1973) was from Naomi Watts' father.

7. Some dudes stole guitars and even Bill Wyman's bass from the rented villa where Rolling Stones recorded "Exile On Main St." (1972).

8. Bassist John Paul Jones almost quit recording "Physical Graffiti" (1975) to become a choirmaster.

9. Patti Smith's "Easter" (1978) was her first album since her infamous stage fall.

10. Bob Dylan had to re-record some songs in "Blood on the Tracks" (1975) after the test acetate pressing.

THE GREATEST

HITS OF 1980S

GREATEST HITS OF 1980S

1. How old was George Michael when he wrote the song "Careless Whisper"?
    a. 19
    b. 17
    c. 18
    d. 20

2. Name the singer who had the hit "John Wayne is Big Leggy" in 1982.
    a. Belouis Some
    b. Culture Club
    c. Hayzi Fantayzee
    d. None of the above

3. ZTT Records was one of the most prominent record companies in the 80s. What does ZTT stand for?
    a. Zany Times Two
    b. Zoo Too Blue
    c. Zoo Too True
    d. Zang Tuum Tumb

4. What do the following artists have in common: Linda McCartney, David Sylvian, and Nick Rhodes?

    a. Amateur golfers

    b. Amateur photographers

    c. Amateur actors/actresses

    d. Amateur dancers

5. How many members were there in the UB40 pop band?

    a. 9

    b. 6

    c. 8

    d. 10

6. Neil Arthur was the lead singer for which group.

    a. Black mania

    b. Blancmange

    c. Icicle Works

    d. China Crisis

7. Which lyrics are these from?

"I'll give you television. I'll give you eyes of blue. I'll give you men who want to rule the world".

    a. Modern Love by David Bowie
    b. Dirty Laundry by Don Henley
    c. Little Red Corvette by Prince
    d. China Girl by David Bowie

8. "Guilty" was a duet hit in 1980 by Barbra Streisand and which singer?

    a. Bryan Adams
    b. Neil Diamond
    c. David Bowie
    d. Barry Gibb

9. Part II of the song "Another brick in the wall" Pink Floyd is about which subject?

    a. love

b. war

c. family

d. school

10. Can you name the most successful album of INXS so far?

    a. Live Baby Live

    b. Kick

    c. Welcome To Wherever You Are

    d. The Swing

11. El Debarge, one of the members of the family group Debarge, had a big hit with which single in 1986?

    a. None of the above

    b. Who's Johnny

    c. Let's go all the way

    d. Rumors

12. The 1985 big hit "The heat is on" by Glenn Frey appeared in a movie. Can you name it?

    a. Beverly Hills Cop

    b. Back To The Future

    c. It did not appear in no movie

    d. Top Gun

13. Can you name the former Metallica member who formed his metal band and the name of his band too?
    a. Dave Mustaine – Megadeth
    b. Lars Ullrich – The Jets
    c. Cliff Burton – Dead Milkmen
    d. Cliff Burton – Iron Strings

14. "Three feet high and rising" was the debut album of which band?
    a. De La Soul
    b. Kim Carnes
    c. Megadeth
    d. Def Leppard

15. Name the band that didn't have a hit in the 80s.
    a. Strawberry Switchblade
    b. The Dream Academy
    c. De La Soul
    d. Backstreet Boys

16. Name the only UK top 5 single by the Belle Stars.
    a. The clapping song
    b. Since yesterday

c. 80's Romance

d. Sign of the times

17. Name the singer who started the song "Do they know it's Christmas" by the Band Aid.
    a. Midge Ure
    b. Bono
    c. David Bowie
    d. Paul Young

18. Name who sung the song by recognizing the song's lyrics: "The first picture of you. The first picture of summer. Seeing the flowers scream their joy".
    a. China Crisis
    b. Kajagoogoo
    c. Backstreet Boys
    d. The Lotus Eaters

19. Status Quo had how many top 20 singles in the 80s?
    a. 16
    b. 14
    c. 18
    d. 12

20. Name the first single that was entirely composed of samples.
    a. Pump up the volume by MARRS
    b. Blue monday by New Order
    c. Good life by Inner City
    d. None of the above

21. What was the only hit single by the Pookah Makes Three?
    a. Champagne Charlie
    b. The way the world is
    c. None of the above
    d. Take it back

22. Big Audio Dynamite was formed in 1985 by which Clash member?
    a. Joe Stummer
    b. Peter Hook
    c. Mick Jones
    d. Topper Headon

23. "Big in Japan" was the debut single of which German band in 1984?
    a. H2O
    b. None of the above

c. Alphaville
d. Ultravox

24. Director Jonathan Demme made a documentary in 1984 about "Stop making sense" – after the last major tour of which band?
   a. Talking Heads
   b. The Jam
   c. Led Zeppelin
   d. Ultravox

25. Which album of U2 featured a cover with the intense stare of a kid?
   a. None of the above
   b. War
   c. The Unforgettable Fire
   d. The Joshua Tree

26. Which rapper featured on the song "I feel for you" by Chaka Khan's?
    a. Fresh Prince
    b. Melle Mel
    c. Chuck D
    d. De La Soul

27. "Why am I playing at both Wembley and Philadelphia? Because I am mad that's why." In 1985, which rock star performed at both the US and UK Live Aid?
    a. David Bowie
    b. Phil Collins
    c. Bob Dylan
    d. Eric Clapton

28. Which teen singer reached number one in 1987 with the song "I think we're alone now"?
    a. Tiffany
    b. Debbie Gibson
    c. Bruce Springsteen
    d. Alannah Myles

29. Buster Bloodvessel was the lead singer for which band?

a. Haircut 100
b. Aerosmith
c. Dead or Alive
d. Bad Manners

30. Their first top 10 single in the UK chart was "To cut a long story short", and the last one was "Through the barricades". Do you know who they are?
    a. China Crisis
    b. Tears For Fears
    c. Spandau Ballet
    d. Culture Club

ANSWER KEY
GREATEST HITS OF THE 1980S

1. B	17. D
2. C	18. D
3. D	19. C
4. B	20. A
5. D	21. D
6. B	22. C
7. D	23. C
8. D	24. A
9. D	25. B
10. B	26. B
11. B	27. B
12. A	28. A
13. A	29. D
14. A	30. C
15. D	
16. D	

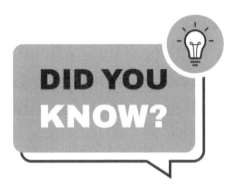

1. Rock and Roll pioneer Bill Haley performed for the last time during a tour of South Africa in June 1980. He died in February 1981.

2. AC/DC released Back in Black (their 7th studio album) in June 1980. This ground-breaking album has sold over 50 million copies worldwide.

3. Led Zeppelin drummer Jon Bonham died in September 1980. The official finding was "accidental death". Bonham was only 32 when he died. Led Zeppelin officially disbanded in December 1980.

4. The list of bands / groups formed in 1981 includes Anthrax, Bananarama, Big Country, Butthole Surfers, Dead Can Dance, Gigolo Aunts, Green Jelly, Metallica, Ministry, Mötley Crüe, Napalm Death, Pantera, Pet Shop Boys, Run-DMC, Scream, Slayer, Sonic Youth, Tears for Fears, Throwing Muses, Wham! and Yazoo.

5. U2 made their first US television appearance on the Tomorrow Show with Tom Snyder in June 1981.

6. MTV started broadcasting in the USA on the 1st of August 1981. They played music videos 24 hours a day.

7. The Buggles song "Video Killed The Radio Star" was the first music video that was played on MTV.

8. In September 1981 Simon & Garfunkel played a free reunion show in Central Park in New York City. More than 500,000 people attended the show.

9. Michael Jackson's Thriller album was released in November 1982. To date the album has sold

more than 110 million copies (making it the greatest selling album of all time). The album reached number 1 on the US charts in 1983. It spent thirty-seven (non-consecutive) weeks at number 1 in the 1980s.

10. Madonna released her debut single "Everybody" on the 1st of November 1982. She only had her first Top 10 hit in 1984 with "Borderline."

THE LEGEND

THE LEGEND

1. What was Elvis' first #1 hit on the U.S. Billboard pop charts?
   a. Heartbreak Hotel
   b. Hound Dog
   c. Stuck on You
   d. Burning Love

2. Name "The Beatles" song that gave them their first US No.1 hit?
   a. "From Me To You"
   b. "I Want To Hold Your Hand"
   c. "She Loves Me"
   d. "In My Life"

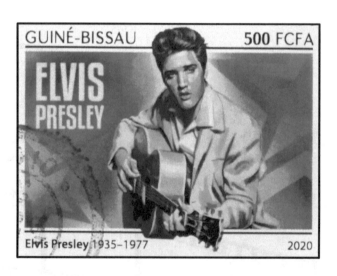

3. What single did Elvis record after suing Priscilla for divorce on January 8, 1973?
    a. Blue Christmas
    b. Separate Ways
    c. All Shook Up
    d. Always on My Mind

4. Elvis memorized every line from what George C. Scott movie?
    a. Strange Love
    b. Patton
    c. Jane Eyre
    d. The Last Run

5. What Elvis hit single was based on an 1861 classical piece entitled "Aura Lee"?
    a. Love Me Tender
    b. Don't Be Cruel
    c. Hard Headed Woman
    d. Are You Lonesome Tonight?

6. What was the first National TV show that Elvis appeared on?
    a. Ed Sullivan Show
    b. Stage Show

c. Tonight Show

d. Ted Mack's Original Amateur Hour

7. What actress did Elvis always send flowers to when she opened a show in Las Vegas?

    a. Ginger Alden

    b. Julie Parrish

    c. Ann-Margaret

    d. Charo

8. What Elvis Presley hit was originally recorded in 1950 by Ernest Tubb?

    a. Blue Christmas

    b. All Shook Up

    c. In The Ghetto

    d. Don't Be Cruel

9. What was the first magazine that ever published an article about Elvis?

    a. Country Song Roundup

    b. Double Dance

    c. Down Beat

    d. Rolling Stone

10. Approximately how many records has Elvis sold worldwide?
    a. Over 150 million
    b. Over 500 million
    c. Over 1 billion
    d. Over 1 trillion

11. Where did Elvis perform all of his rock concerts?
    a. North America
    b. Europe
    c. South America
    d. Asia

12. Which song helped Elvis win his first Grammy?
    a. How Great Thou Art
    b. Don't Be Cruel
    c. She Thinks I Still Care
    d. I Forgot to Remember to Forget

13. How many songs did Elvis Presley record?
    a. Around 300 songs.
    b. Around 500 songs.
    c. Around 710 songs.
    d. Around 850 songs.

14. How many years was he active as a musician?

    a. 8

    b. 10

    c. 19

    d. 24

15. At what age did Elvis make his first record?

    a. 18

    b. 21

    c. 22

    d. 25

ANSWER KEY

THE LEGEND

1. A
2. B
3. B
4. B
5. A
6. B
7. C
8. A
9. A
10. C
11. A
12. A
13. C
14. D
15. A

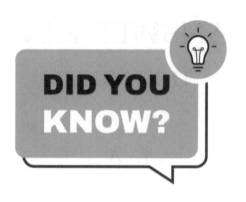

He Grew Up Dirt Poor

Although he'd one day become music royalty, little Elvis grew up absolutely dirt poor. His father, Vernon, was not the ambitious sort, and could barely hold down a job. Elvis and his mother Gladys paid the price for Vernon's pitiful breadwinning attempts, often relying on the neighbors or the government for food and support.

He Lost His Home

In 1938, Elvis's father was charged with altering his landlord's check and sentenced to eight months in prison—but this stint had even more devastating consequences. It forced Elvis and his mother to give up their home. Although they found refuge with some relatives, poverty plagued Elvis throughout his childhood.

He Was Extremely Shy

At school, Elvis was exceedingly average. He was painfully shy and none of his accomplishments made him a standout student. He hadn't yet discovered an affinity for music. However, that was about to change. As a first-grader, he impressed his teacher with a rendition of "Old Shep" during morning prayers—so much so that she pushed him to enter a singing contest at a local fair.

He Couldn't Read Music

Although Elvis had an undeniable passion for music, he couldn't actually read music. Instead he played by ear and learned as much as he could from the music he loved. His inspiration came from a multitude of places. He adored country artists like Hank Snow, and frequently visited record shops, swaying to the melodies that poured from the jukeboxes.

THE UNBEATABLE

BEATLES

THE UNBEATABLE BEATLES

1. On the famous album cover, which Beatle crossed Abbey Road first?
    a. George
    b. Paul
    c. John
    d. Ringo

2. "In the town where I was born, lived a man who sailed to sea" is the start of which Beatles classic?
    a. Penny Lane
    b. Yellow Submarine
    c. Strawberry Fields Forever
    d. Ticket To Ride

3. The Beatles debut single went to no.1 in 1964 in the USA. What was it called?
   a. I Saw Her Standing There
   b. Love Me Do
   c. Can't Buy Me Love
   d. A Hard Day's Night

4. Who was the first drummer for The Beatles?
   a. Pete Best
   b. Pete Bancroft
   c. Pete Barlow
   d. Pete Bell

5. Which classic song suggests you "take a sad song and make it better"?
   a. Eight Days A Week
   b. Day Tripper
   c. Yesterday
   d. Hey Jude

6. Where did The Beatles final live concert take place on 29 August 1966?
   a. Candlestick Park, San Francisco
   b. Wembley Stadium, London
   c. Hollywood Bowl, Los Angeles
   d. Madison Square Garden, New York

7. Which of the Beatles did some fans believe had died and been replaced by a double?
    a. Paul
    b. George
    c. John
    d. Ringo

8. What band did Ringo leave to join the Beatles?
    a. Tony Sheridan & The Beat Brothers
    b. Alan Caldwell & The Stoneycraft Storm
    c. Rory Storm & The Hurricanes
    d. Johnny & The Moondogs

9. Which of the following songs contributed to the rumor that Paul had died?
    a. Penny Lane
    b. Strawberry Fields Forever
    c. Hey Jude
    d. Yesterday

10. Why did George Martin make the Beatles rerecord "Please Please Me"?
    a. It was too slow.
    b. John Lennon was sick.
    c. The lyrics were too explicit.
    d. The drumming was subpar.

11. Which album required over 700 hours of recordings?
    a. Sgt. Pepper's Lonely Heart Club Band
    b. Let It Be
    c. White Album
    d. Abbey Road

12. In what Beatles song did George Harrison first play the sitar?
    a. I'm Looking Through You
    b. Across The Universe
    c. Within You, Without You
    d. Norwegian Wood

13. What is the only song John Lennon recorded completely by himself during his time with the Beatles?
    a. Mother

b. Julia

c. In My Life

d. Only A Northern Song

14. What was the Beatles' first single to sell a million copies?

    a. Hey Jude

    b. I Want To Hold Your Hand

    c. Can't But Me Love

    d. She Loves You

15. Why did the BBC ban I Am the Walrus?

    a. Use of the word 'knickers'.

    b. Peta Protests.

    c. It was just too weird.

    d. Drug references.

ANSWER KEY

THE UNBEATABLE BEATLES

1. C

2. B

3. B

4. A

5. D

6. A

7. A

8. C

9. B

10. A

11. A

12. D

13. B

14. D

15. A

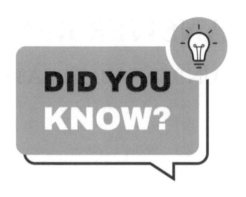

The Beatles Used To Live In A Cinema

The Beatles didn't always live in the lap of luxury; at the beginning they lived in Hamburg from 1960-1962, but when they first arrived, they lived in a cinema. Lennon commented on his experience there: 'We would go to bed late and be woken up the next day by the sound of the cinema show.

Hey Jules

But did you know that it wasn't originally written about someone called Jude? It was in fact initially called Hey Jules and aimed at Lennon's five year old son Julian. 'Hey Jules, don't make it bad…'

Ready To Rock & Roll

The song Yesterday apparently came to McCartney in a dream completely formed and ready to record. The Beatle was so surprised by how easily it had come to him that he had to ask friends 'Is this by me or did someone else write it?' The song's catchy title however was originally called something else entirely – Scrambled Eggs.

Their Concerts Often Smelled Like Urine

The masses of young girls who turned up for concerts, movie premieres, or to wave hello as the Beatles walked off the plane in a new city were apparently too distracted by their love for the lads to care about whether or not their bladders were full.

They Recorded Their First Album In One Day

Following the success of "Please Please Me" as a single, the record company wanted a full album as soon as possible. So, George Martin capitalized on the wild, live energy the boys perfected in Hamburg and recorded the entire Please Please Me LP in less than 13 hours — saving "Twist and Shout" for last so the taxing vocals wouldn't ruin Lennon's voice before the other songs were done.

ROCK IT WITH

BOB DYLAN

ROCK IT WITH BOB DYLAN

1. Dylan's 1969 double-LP, widely considered rock's first bootleg album, was titled:
    a. "The White Album"
    b. "The Basement Tapes"
    c. "The Black Album"
    d. "Great White Wonder"

2. This album was the first of a trilogy reflecting Dylan's spiritual awakening.
    a. "Saved"
    b. "Oh Mercy"
    c. "Shot of Love"
    d. "Slow Train Coming"

3. Who first had a hit record with a Dylan composition?
   a. Joan Baez
   b. Peter, Paul and Mary
   c. The Byrds
   d. The Beatles

4. Which album did Bob Dylan himself describe as 'that wild mercury sound'?
   a. Highway 61 Revisited
   b. Blonde On Blonde
   c. Blood On The Tracks
   d. Another Side of Dylan

5. Which American folk singer was Bob Dylan greatly influenced by?
   a. Pete Seeger
   b. Cisco Houston
   c. Ben Harper
   d. Woody Guthrie

6. Which song was the first that Bob Dylan sang on TV?
   a. Man of Constant Sorrow
   b. Like a Rolling Stone

c. Blowin' in the Wind

d. The Times They Are Changin'

7. Which of these records did start the Bob Dylan's Rock Period?
    a. Highway 61 Revisited
    b. Bringing it All Back Home
    c. Blonde on Blonde
    d. Another Side Of Bob Dylan

8. Which Biblical characters are mentioned in Bob Dylan's song "Desolation Row"?
    a. Noah And Ham
    b. Abraham And Joseph
    c. David And Goliath
    d. Cain And Abel

9. Why was Bob Dylan criticized at the Newport Folk Festival?
    a. He Used An Electric Guitar
    b. He Mumbled His Words
    c. He Refused To Play
    d. He Did Not Use The Harmonica

10. According to a certain Bob Dylan song, what is a good car to drive after a war?
    a. Lincoln
    b. Mercedes
    c. Cadillac
    d. Mercury

ANSWER KEY
ROCK IT WITH BOB DYLAN

1. D

2. D

3. B

4. B

5. D

6. A

7. B

8. D

9. A

10. C

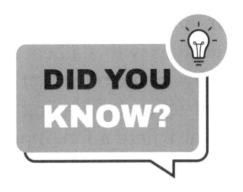

For a long time in 1966, fans thought he had died.

On July 29, 1966, Dylan crashed his Triumph motorbike on the back roads around Woodstock, NY. As one of the major artists of the time, and a vocal protester on the social scene, fans had no idea where he'd gone.

Years later, the star acknowledged that he'd been exhausted. He'd just wound down an extensive tour, his drug use was out of control, and he was dealing with stalkers and plagued by obsessive fans. Some reports at the time say that Dylan had taken to sleeping with a gun, after an incident where a fan approached him with a rifle.

His wife was a Playboy Bunny.

Dylan's wife, Sara Lownds—who inspired the song, 'Sara,' from the Desire album—was a former Playboy bunny and model, an interesting fact about Bob Dylan. When the pair married in 1965, Sara appealed to Dylan's desire to live a quiet, non-celebrity life. She represented a change for the artist, and he credited her with offering a calm energy and presence in the hurricane that was his adult life.

Dylan's wife, Sara Lownds—who inspired the song, 'Sara,' from the Desire album—was a former Playboy bunny and model, an interesting fact about Bob Dylan. When the pair married in 1965, Sara appealed to Dylan's desire to live a quiet, non-celebrity life. She represented a change for the artist, and he credited her with offering a calm energy and presence in the hurricane that was his adult life.

THE KING OF POP

THE KING OF POP

1. What dance craze did Michael popularize in 1983?
   a. The Running Man
   b. The Robot
   c. The Moonwalk
   d. The Floss

2. Which Michael Jackson music video features dancing zombies?
   a. Bad
   b. Man in the Mirror
   c. Thriller
   d. Beat It

3. Michael was known for wearing a rhinestone _____.
   a. Mask
   b. Hat
   c. Glove
   d. Vest

4. Which Michael Jackson music video was the most expensive to produce?

a. Scream
b. Black of White
c. Thriller
d. Bad

5. What was the first song Michael ever sang in public?
    a. Monster Mash
    b. Climb Every Mountain
    c. I Saw Mommy Kissing Santa Claus
    d. Gary, Indiana

6. For which music video did Jackson develop a gravity-defying lean?
    a. Smooth Criminal
    b. Bad
    c. Scream
    d. Beat It

7. Whose music catalog did Jackson purchase the rights to in 1985?
    a. The Beatles
    b. Ella Fitzgerald
    c. Diana Ross
    d. The Rolling Stones

8. In which song does Michael sing: "It doesn't matter who's wrong or right"?
    a. The Girl is Mine
    b. Beat It
    c. Bad
    d. Billie Jean

9. What concert tour was Jackson rehearsing for when he died?
    a. This is It
    b. End of the World
    c. The Final Curtain
    d. The End Has Come

10. In which song does Michael sing: "If this town is just an apple, then let me take a bite"?
    a. Human Nature
    b. Don't Stop 'Til You Get Enough
    c. Wanna Be Startin' Somethin'
    d. The Girl is Mine

11. How many copies has the album Thriller sold worldwide?
    a. 20 million
    b. 50 million

c. 75 million

d. over 100 million

12. Whom did Michael Jackson teach to dance in the video for Jam?
    a. Eddie Murphy
    b. Shaquille O'Neal
    c. John Travolta
    d. Michael Jordan

13. Michael Jackson contributed a song to which movie soundtrack?
    a. E.T.
    b. Indiana Jones
    c. Star Wars
    d. Ghost Busters

14. What is the name of the 1985 single Michael Jackson co-wrote with Lionel Richie to help raise funds for famine-relief efforts in Africa?
    a. Tears Are Not Enough
    b. Do They Know It's Christmas?
    c. We Are The World
    d. One More Day

15. Michael Jackson wrote several songs while sitting in a favorite tree. What name did he give this tree?
    a. The Thoughtful Tree
    b. The Giving Tree
    c. The Inspiration Tree
    d. The Epiphany Tree

16. What is the name of the single Michael Jackson wrote for Hurricane Katrina victims?
    a. What More Can I Give
    b. I Have This Dream
    c. Heal The World
    d. Man In The Mirror

17. What famous guitarist played on Michael Jackson's "Beat It"?
    a. Steve Stevens
    b. Slash
    c. Carlos Santana
    d. Eddie Van Halen

18. Which Michael Jackson video was recognized by the Guinness Book of World

Records as "The Most Successful Music Video of All Time"?

    a. Bad
    b. Beat It
    c. Scream
    d. Thriller

19. In 1985, how much money did Michael Jackson pay for the publishing rights to the Beatles catalogue?

    a. $25 million
    b. $35 million
    c. $47.5 million
    d. $51.5 million

20. In what year did Michael Jackson receive his star on the Hollywood Walk of Fame?

    a. 1991
    b. 1989
    c. 1984
    d. 1978

ANSWER KEY

THE KING OF POP

1. C
2. C
3. C
4. A
5. B
6. A
7. A
8. B
9. A
10. A
11. D
12. D

13. A
14. C
15. B
16. B
17. D
18. D
19. C
20. C

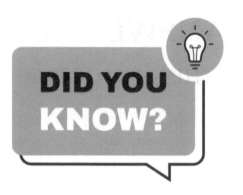

He made $2 billion in his lifetime... and blew it all

Despite making $1.1 billion – or $2 billion, adjusted for inflation – in his lifetime, Jackson was such a big spender that he burned through it all. At the end of his life, Jackson, despite his enormous earnings, had around $350 million worth of debt to his name.

Thriller is the best-selling album of all time

Among the many accolades the record won, Thriller took eight Grammys and became the first album to go 30x platinum. Thriller ended up spending 122 weeks on the Billboard 200 in the US, and at its peak sold 1 million copies in just one week. Perhaps unsurprisingly, the album is now the best-selling of all time, with 66 million units sold.

Billie Jean is based on a true story

According to a top Jackson biographer, Billie Jean was in fact a real person who wrote to Michael claiming that he had fathered her twins. Jackson himself, however, claimed that 'Billie Jean' was a composite of several women who claimed their children were fathered by Michael's brothers while he was on the road with the Jackson 5.

His music video for Scream is the most expensive of all time

At a cost of $7 million, "Scream" was listed in Guinness World Records as the most expensive music video ever made ($6 million more than "Thriller"). It won three MTV Video Music Awards and the Grammy Award for Best Music Video.

He was such an animal enthusiast that he bought his own zoo

As a child, Jackson was an animal lover, with a particular affinity for German Shepherds and a pet rat, named Ben, who he wrote his first ever song about.

Neverland Ranch was Jackson's home as well as his private amusement park, with a Ferris wheel, Carousel, Zipper, Octopus, Pirate Ship, Wave Swinger, Super Slide, roller coaster, bumper cars, an amusement arcade, and a petting zoo. He named the property after an island in J. M. Barrie's Peter Pan, the story of a boy who never grows up.

His trademark

More than the black fedora, the white socks and loafers, or the red leather jacket, the solitary white rhinestone glove -- made famous when he premiered the moonwalk in 1983 -- became a Jackson trademark. The original glove was later auctioned off for $350,000.

THE ROLLING

STONES

THE ROLLING STONES

1. Which blues singer were the Rolling Stones named after?
   a. Muddy Waters
   b. Elmore James
   c. B.B. King
   d. John Lee Hooker

2. Which goddess inspired the Rolling Stones' logo?
   a. Isis
   b. Freya
   c. Kali
   d. Athena

3. Why did Ed Sullivan ban the Rolling Stones from his show?
   a. They set the dressing room on fire.
   b. Their fans were too loud.
   c. Their hair was too long.
   d. They refused to edit their lyrics.

4. In which song does Mick Jagger sing: "I shouted out 'Who killed the Kennedys?' when after all, it was you and me"?
    a. Beast of Burden
    b. You Can't Always Get What You Want
    c. Sympathy for the Devil
    d. Paint It Black

5. Which Stones hit was originally intended as a B-side?
    a. Paint It Black
    b. Wild Horses
    c. (I Can't Get No) Satisfaction
    d. Sympathy for the Devil

6. Which cocktail was popularized by the Rolling Stones?
    a. Mint Julep
    b. Tequila Sunrise
    c. White Russian
    d. Cosmopolitan

7. Which member of the Rolling Stones was a Boy Scout?
    a. Keith Richards
    b. Charlie Watts
    c. Ronnie Wood
    d. Mick Jagger

8. In which song does Mick Jagger sing: "With no lovin' in our souls and no money in our coats, you can't say we're satisfied"?
    a. Angie
    b. (I Can't Get No) Satisfaction
    c. 19th Nervous Breakdown
    d. Honky Tonk Women

9. What pseudonym was used for songs written by the entire band?
   a. Maarten Maartens
   b. Andrej Zivor
   c. Nanker Phelge
   d. Blaise Cendrars

10. Which Beatles song did Mick Jagger sing backup on?
   a. Baby, You're A Rich Man
   b. With A Little Help From My Friends
   c. Getting Better
   d. Fixing A Hole

11. Which member of the Rolling Stones studied ballet?
   a. Ronnie Wood
   b. Mick Jagger
   c. Charlie Watts
   d. Keith Richards

12. Which original member of the band was kicked out before the Rolling Stones took off?
   a. Ian Stewart
   b. Mick Taylor

c. Billy Preston

d. Brian Jones

13. Which band member doesn't like to sleep?
    a. Ronnie Wood
    b. Mick Jagger
    c. Charlie Watts
    d. Keith Richards

14. Which band member once punched Mick Jagger in the face?
    a. Ronnie Wood
    b. Billy Wyman
    c. Charlie Watts
    d. Keith Richards

15. Which actor mocked the Stones' music and hair after a variety show performance in 1964?
    a. Dean Martin
    b. Bob Hope
    c. Frank Sinatra
    d. John Wayne

ANSWER KEY

THE ROLLING STONES

1. A

2. C

3. B

4. C

5. C

6. B

7. A

8. A

9. C

10. A

11. B

12. A

13. D

14. C

15. A

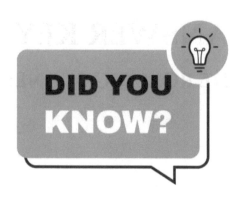

1. Charlie Watts secretly wed Shirley Ann Shepherd, a plasterer's daughter, on October 14, 1964. He tried to keep it a secret because the group thought he should stay a bachelor. Watts explained, "I tried to keep it a secret. I wanted it to be a secret. But I suppose if Kruschev can't keep a secret, neither can I."

2. Fourteen hotels turned the band down when they tried to find a comfortable bed in New York City for their American tour in June and July 1966. This wasn't just because of their reputation as short-tempered hotel room wreckers. It was also because of the increasing difficulties of keeping the fans at bay.

3. Keith Richards failed his driving test three times and sent his minder instead to impersonate him. The minder eventually passed on Richards' behalf.

4. Jean Shrimpton had a fling first with Keith Richards, then with Brian Jones, and then settled down with Mick Jagger.

5. It was a slippery slope for Brian Jones and drugs. By 1966, he had become obsessed with devouring celebs and fame and attention. On tour, Jones was by now drinking one and a half liters of whiskey a day. He was popping pills by the handful, "downers" as well as amyl nitrite, and thoroughly enjoyed his hallucinogens – peyote, acid, mushrooms and whatever else was close to hand.

6. Mick Jagger doesn't shy away from diaper duty. In fact, he's quite good at it. "I've always changed nappies, for other people's children as well as my own," he said. "I change[d] Ronnie Wood's children's nappies. You do these things when it's necessary – although I'm not about to

become a full-time house-husband like John Lennon did at one stage [but] I'm relatively experienced and I quite enjoy it."

7. Mick Jagger's raunchy blockbuster, "She's The Boss," (released in 1985) in which he appeared in drag, set the rocker back a staggering £30,000 in frocks, frills, powder and paint – and that was just for his costume. Later Jagger admitted that he was "still the sexiest bit of skirt around."

8. Ronnie Wood never had an affair with Margaret Trudeau, the wife of Canada' Prime Minister, Pierre Trudeau. She did however, he admits, "boogie with them" for a couple of days while the band was on tour.

9. Bill Wyman, the bass guitarist, has kept a diary of the group ever since they started in 1961. He has written over 22,000 words stored on four computers. He planned to write an inside story of the most raunchy band pop has ever known.

FRANK SINATRA

FRANK SINATRA

1. How did he learn to read music?
    a. Having private lessons
    b. In musical school
    c. He never learned to read music
    d. Influence from parents

2. What is Frank's voice type?
    a. Tenor
    b. Countertenor
    c. Bass
    d. Baritone

3. Which movie made him win an Oscar?
    a. Paris When It Sizzles
    b. High Society

  c. Meet Me in Las Vegas

  d. From Here to Eternity

4. What was his last album?

  a. On The Air

  b. A Swingin' Affair!

  c. Duets II

  d. Come Fly With Me

5. What's the name of the record label founded by Frank Sinatra?

  a. Easy Star Records

  b. Reprise Records

  c. Arista Records

  d. Star Records

6. Can you tell how many of Frank Sinatra's records have been sold worldwide?

  a. Over 50 million

  b. Over 100 million

  c. Over 150 million

  d. Over 200 million

7. What was his nickname?
   a. The Chairman of the Board
   b. The voice
   c. The Sultan of Swoon
   d. Ol' Green eyes

8. What were the words of Frank Sinatra?
   a. "A person has learned much when he has learned how to die."
   b. "I'm losing it."
   c. "Get busy living, or get busy dying."
   d. "Six feet of earth makes us all equal."

9. What was the cause of his death?
   a. Pneumonia
   b. Heart attack
   c. Suicide
   d. Cancer

10. Can you tell the name of his favorite drink?
    a. two fingers of whiskey with four ice cubes and a splash of water
    b. two fingers of bourbon with a splash of honey
    c. Vodka on the rocks
    d. Tequila

ANSWER KEY

FRANK SINATRA

1. C

2. D

3. D

4. A

5. B

6. C

7. D

8. B

9. B

10. A

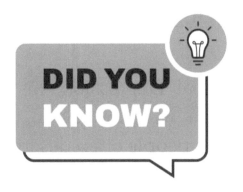

His birth left him with lifelong scars.

Sinatra was a big baby, a hefty 13.5 lbs at the time of his birth and had to be delivered with the aid of forceps, which left him with severe scars on his left cheek, neck and ear. It also perforated his eardrum, leaving them damaged for the rest of his life.

A later operation on his mastoid bone left him with major scarring on his neck. All his life, Sinatra hated to be photographed from the left side.

He was a well-dressed kid during the Great Depression.

During the Great Depression, his mother often supplied Sinatra with money to buy expensive clothes. For this, people often described him as the "best-dressed kid in the neighborhood." Throughout his life, Sinatra would continue to be known for his impeccable sense of style.

He was arrested and charged for seduction and adultery.

In 1938, Sinatra was arrested in New Jersey for seduction. He was later charged with adultery when it was determined that the woman was actually married. The case was eventually dismissed.

His punctured eardrum kept him out of World War II.

On December 11, 1943, he was officially classified 4-F ("Registrant not acceptable for military service") by the draft board because of his perforated eardrum. Towards the end of the war,

Sinatra joined several overseas USO tours to help entertain the troops.

His son, Frank Sinatra, Jr., was kidnapped and held for ransom.

On December 8, 1963, Sinatra received a ransom demand of $240,000 for the safe return of his son. The kidnappers only allowed Sinatra to call from a payphone. During one call, Sinatra ran out of money in the middle of the call. He was horrified that the error would cost him his son's life. After the payment was made and Frank, Jr. was safely returned, Sinatra always carried a roll of dimes, vowing to never be without coins again.

The FBI kept him under surveillance for almost five decades.

Beginning in the 1940s, the FBI kept a close eye on Sinatra due to his alleged ties to the mafia. The Feds kept over two thousand documents on the singer. Although Sinatra denied any involvement, his rumored association with the mob never abated.

He was a close friend of President John F. Kennedy.

Sinatra had helped campaign for Kennedy during his presidential run. A version of Sinatra's song "High Hopes" was used as Kennedy's campaign song. However, the friends had a falling out before Kennedy's death due to Sinatra's alleged mafia connections. When he learned of Kennedy's assassination, Sinatra reportedly cried for days in his bedroom.

THE ROCKIN'

JIMI HENDRIX

THE ROCKIN' JIMI HENDRIX

1. What guitarist claims he's seen Jimi Hendrix's ghost?
    a. Robin Trower
    b. Dave Mason
    c. Ulrich Roth
    d. Yngwie Malmsteen

2. Jimi Hendrix would have been found using which of these amplifiers?
    a. Marshall Plexi Reissue
    b. Boogie
    c. Marshall Plexi
    d. Fender Tweet Blues

3. Which is a Dylan song that was covered by Jimi Hendrix?
    a. Hey Joe
    b. All Along The Watchtower
    c. Knockin' On Heaven's Door
    d. Mr. Tambourine Man

4. What did Jimi Hendrix and Dick Dale have in common?
    a. They Both Played Left Handed
    b. They Both Went To UCLA
    c. They Both Are From Seattle
    d. They Both Played Les Pauls

5. Who wrote Jimi Hendrix's "Hey Joe"?
    a. Billy Roberts
    b. Noel Redding
    c. Jimi Hendrix
    d. Billy Cox

6. Who did Jimi Hendrix write the song "The Wind Cries Mary" for?
    a. Janis Joplin
    b. Eric Clapton
    c. Kathy Etchingham
    d. Monika Danneman

7. Who sings backing vocals on the Jimi Hendrix song "Earth Blues"?
    a. The Ronnettes
    b. Buddy Miles
    c. Noel Redding
    d. The Ghetto Fighters

8. The Jimi Hendrix song, "Dolly Dagger" is about which of Jimi's girlfriends?
    a. Monika Danneman
    b. Linda Kieth
    c. Kathy Etchingham
    d. Devon White

9. Which of these songs did Jimi Hendrix write first?
    a. 51st Anniversary
    b. Purple Haze

c. Hey Joe

d. Stone Free

10. Which of these songs did Hendrix drummer Mitch Mitchell write?

    a. Beginnings

    b. Earth Blues

    c. Little Miss Strange

    d. 51st Anniversary

11. What was the typing error on one of Jimi Hendrix's demo albums?

    a. The Jimmy Hendricks Experience

    b. The Star Spangled Banter

    c. Purple Hayes

    d. Electric Landlady

12. Which legendary blues guitarist put Jimi Hendrix down for his style of playing the blues?

    a. Howlin' Wolf

    b. Muddy Waters

    c. B.B. King

    d. John Lee Hooker

13. Who inspired Jimi Hendrix's classic song "Manic Depression"?
    a. Mitch Mitchell
    b. Mike Jeffery
    c. Noel Redding
    d. Chas Chandler

14. Who of the following did Jimi Hendrix never play or jam with?
    a. Brian Jones
    b. Ginger Baker
    c. Tina Turner
    d. George Harrison

15. What was the last song Jimi Hendrix performed at Woodstock?
    a. Hey Joe
    b. Wild Thing
    c. Fire
    d. Voodoo Child

ANSWER KEY

THE ROCKIN' JIMI HENDRIX

1. B
2. C
3. B
4. A
5. A
6. C
7. A
8. D
9. D
10. A
11. D
12. A
13. B
14. D
15. A

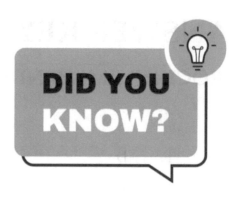

Jimi Hendrix's background history is very interesting

The first instrument Jimi tried was a ukulele, and he was soon trying to convince his dad to buy him a guitar.

Jimi Hendrix's dad encouraged his talents in music

Jimi Hendrix's dad bought him his first guitar when he was only 15 years old. A year later, Al bought Jimi his second guitar which was an electric guitar.

An interesting fact about Jimi Hendrix is that he was self-taught and he couldn't even read music. Despite this, he succeeded and became one of the greatest guitar players that have ever existed.

It has been said that Hendrix used to play his guitar upside-down because he was left-handed and it was much easier for him to play this way.

Jimi Hendrix had a volatile temperament

At the Monterey Pop Festival, which happened in 1967, Jimi Hendrix set his guitar on fire, and he was truly happy to do so.

His shows were always filled with energy and that's why his fans loved him so much. He created a performance that would never be forgotten.

He headlined many festivals, and he played over 600 shows all over the world from 1966 to 1970.

STEVIE WONDER

STEVIE WONDER

1. What was Stevie Wonder's birth name?
   a. Steven Wonet Dervan
   b. Stevenia Wondovia
   c. Stephen Emmanuel Haskins
   d. Steveland Hardaway Judkins

2. How did Stevie Wonder lose his eyesight?
   a. He was born blind.
   b. Early macular degeneration.
   c. He was involved in an accident.
   d. The conditions in his premature birth incubator.

3. What age did Stevie Wonder achieve his first US number one single with Fingertips?
   a. 17
   b. 31
   c. 23
   d. 13

4. Which major hit for Smokey Robinson and the Miracles did Wonder write in 1967?
   a. Tears of a Clown
   b. What's So Good About Goodbye
   c. I Don't Blame You At All
   d. Love Machine

5. What was the name of Stevie Wonder's big 1972 album, featuring the No. 1 hit Superstition?
   a. Dancing Vinyl
   b. Talking Book
   c. Reading Record
   d. Superstitious Pages

6. Which major British rock'n roll band did Wonder tour with in the early 70s?
   a. The Who

b. Beatles

c. Kinks

d. Rolling Stones

7. For how many consecutive weeks did Stevie's classic album Songs in the Key of Life stay at number one in the US?
   a. Twenty-eight.
   b. Ten.
   c. Two.
   d. Thirteen.

8. How many Grammy awards has Wonder won in his life?
   a. 10
   b. 20
   c. 25
   d. 15

9. What was the title of the song Stevie Wonder sang at age 11?
   a. It's you
   b. Love them
   c. Lonely boy
   d. You can

10. What effect did the accident Stevie Wonder had in 1973 have on him?
    a. Loss of his memory
    b. Loss of his life
    c. Partial loss of smell and taste sense
    d. Loss of his limbs

ANSWER KEY
STEVIE WONDER

1. D

2. D

3. D

4. A

5. B

6. D

7. D

8. C

9. C

10. C

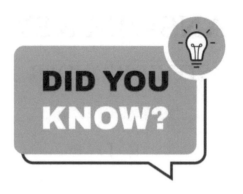

Stevie Wonder wasn't born Blind.

In an interview with Larry King, Stevie Wonder stated that he wasn't born blind. A major cause of Wonder's blindness was an overabundance of oxygen he experienced as an infant in a hospital incubator. This was an accident on the part of the hospital, which coupled with being six weeks premature resulted in Wonder becoming permanently blind.

As a result of a 1973 car crash, Stevie Wonder temporarily lost his sense of smell and taste.

On August 6, 1973, Stevie Wonder was in a car accident. The crash left Wonder in a coma for four days and ultimately resulted in him losing both his sense of smell and taste for a short time. In a twist of fate, exactly 15 years later on to the date, Wonder was gifted with a son named Kwame.

He was the youngest solo artist to have a #1 song on Billboard.

In 51 years, no one has come close to the record Stevie Wonder achieved when he was only 13. As Little Stevie Wonder, his song, "Fingertips – Part 2", reached #1 on the Billboard Top 100, making him the youngest artist to do so. The track simultaneously became the #1 R&B song in the country — also a first.

He performed "Superstition" on Sesame Street.

"Superstition" is one of Wonder's best and most popular songs. For that reason, it's not a surprise he performed the track on Sesame Street. However, what is surprising is how intact Wonder keeps the original composition.

Stevie Wonder's Eivets Rednow is actually "Stevie Wonder" spelled backward.

Stevie Wonder's 1968 easy-listening album, Eivets Rednow, saw the legendary artist play harmonica, drums, piano, and clavinet, though he does not sing. Marking his ninth studio album, Eivets Rednow was actually his first album with songs credited solely to Wonder alone. However, the name of the album comes from spelling "Stevie Wonder" backwards, something that many fans missed initially, causing several reissues to have "How do you spell Stevie Wonder backwards?" to be printed on the album sleeve.

Stevie Wonder's single, "Happy Birthday," is a big reason why Martin Luther King Jr's birthday is a National Holiday.

In 1981, Wonder, along with many other supporters, were rallying for the government to recognize Martin Luther King Jr.'s birthday as a national holiday. "Happy Birthday" was Wonder's way of spreading the word. He even helped organize the Rally for Peace Conference in 1981. President Ronald Reagan would ultimately approve the holiday thanks to these efforts two years later.

FUN OLDIES MUSIC

FUN OLDIES MUSIC

1. Where did Fats Domino find his thrill?
   a. At the roadhouse
   b. On Blueberry Hill
   c. At the tavern
   d. At the drive-in

2. Queen, certainly a group considered to be rock royalty, had a hit with what song in 1975?
   a. Feel Like Makin' Love
   b. Fame
   c. Bohemian Rhapsody
   d. Island Girl

3. Which of these '60s bands sang "California Dreamin'"?
   a. The Ronettes
   b. The Beatles
   c. The Doors
   d. The Mamas and the Papas

4. Who was the lead singer for the Doors in the 1960s?
   a. Jim Morrison
   b. Ray Davies
   c. Robert Plant
   d. Keith Relf

5. Which of these bands was the first to make use of a billboard to advertise a new album release?
   a. The Doors
   b. The Beatles
   c. The Shadows
   d. Led Zeppelin

6. Can you name the country star known to his legions of fans as "The Man in Black"?
   a. Waylon Jennings
   b. Kris Kristofferson

c. Johnny Cash

d. Willie Nelson

7. "Hotel California," a massive hit in 1977, was recorded by which of the bands below?

a. Led Zeppelin

b. Cheap Trick

c. Sweet

d. The Eagles

8. Who died alongside J.P. "The Big Bopper" Richardson and Ritchie Valens in a plane crash on February 3, 1959?

a. Carl Perkins

b. Chet Atkins

c. Buddy Holly

d. Bobby Rydell

9. What rebellious form of music gained traction in the 1970s?

a. Punk

b. Disco

c. Ska

d. Reggae

10. Don McLean famously referenced the death of Buddy Holly, J.P. "The Big Bopper" Richardson and Ritchie Valens in his song "American Pie." What did he call the event?
    a. Teary-eyed serenade
    b. Holly, Valens and the Bopper are gone
    c. That shameful day
    d. The day the music died

11. True or false? The term "rock and roll" was first used to describe a musical genre by disc jockey Alan Freed.
    a. True
    b. False

12. The lyrics, "All of my life, I've been a-waitin', tonight there'll be no hesitatin'," are found in which Buddy Holly song?
    a. "Peggy Sue"
    b. "Oh, Boy!"
    c. "Rave On"
    d. "That'll Be the Day"

13. What is the birth name of Freddie Mercury of Queen?
    a. Georgios Kyriacos Panayiotou

b. Farrokh Bulsara

c. Lewis Allen Reed

d. Robert Allen Zimmerman

14. Can you name the massive music festival that began on August 15, 1969?
    a. Lollapalooza
    b. Woodstock
    c. Glastonbury
    d. Knebworth

15. About how many people attended Woodstock?
    a. 400,000
    b. 15,000
    c. 1 million
    d. 50,000

16. Chuck Berry started making music to fund equipment for his dream job. What was it?
    a. Photographer
    b. Cook
    c. Fisherman
    d. Jockey

17. David Bowie's real name is what?

a. Reginald Kenneth Dwight
b. David Robert Jones
c. Brian Molko
d. Farrokh Bulsara

18. Paul Hewson is the lead singer with U2, an Irish band formed in 1976. What is he more popularly known as?
a. The Ox
b. The Edge
c. Aladdin Sane
d. Bono

19. Released by Chuck Berry in 1958, which song essentially made him famous?
a. "Blueberry Hill"
b. "Tutti Frutti"
c. "Johnny B. Goode"
d. "Roll Over Beethoven"

20. A band in the 1950s with Danny Rapp on lead vocals was known as what?
    a. Danny and the Juniors
    b. Danny and the Crickets
    c. Danny and the Comets
    d. Danny and the Beatles

ANSWER KEY

FUN OLDIES MUSIC

1. B

2. C

3. D

4. A

5. A

6. C

7. D

8. C

9. A

10. D

11. A

12. B

13. B

14. B

15. A

16. A

17. B

18. D

19. C

20. A

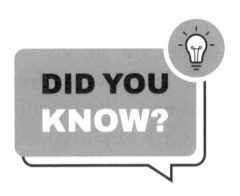

WOODSTOCK WAS BANNED FROM ITS ORIGINAL SITE BECAUSE OF TOILETS.

Woodstock was conceived in early 1969 by a group of twenty-somethings: Artie Kornfeld, Michael Lang, Joel Rosenman, and John Roberts. In January of that year, the four men—Kornfeld and Lang as music industry vets and Rosenman and Roberts as venture capitalists who provided the financial backing— formed the company Woodstock Ventures, named for the New York town that Kornfeld and Lang were scouting to build a recording studio in. Woodstock had long been known as an artists' retreat about two hours north of New York City, and even has its own "Artists Cemetery" for a variety of creative types.

The original site of the festival was intended to be at Howard Mills Industrial Park in Wallkill, near Middletown, New York. After negotiations with landowners, the four believed they had found a solution. But Wallkill residents shot the idea down, fearing that an influx of visitors — possibly under the influence of alcohol or drugs — would be potentially problematic. By insisting the concert's portable toilets weren't up to code and refusing to grant a permit, Wallkill effectively banned Woodstock from taking place there just a month before its scheduled August 15 start date.

WOODSTOCK WAS SAVED BY A FARMER.

When Wallkill fell through, promoters turned to Bethel, New York, a small town with just 2366 residents where a farmer named Max Yasgur owned a 600-acre dairy farm. As in Wallkill, Bethel residents were not terribly enthusiastic about hosting a concert that would attract a considerable crowd. But Yasgur didn't share their apprehensions. Even though he was middle-aged, blue-collar, and as far from a "hippie" as he could be, he respected the desire of concert-goers to share in a communal experience and allowed organizers the use of his property for a fee of $50,000. He even came out at one point to address the crowd (above), congratulating them on the assembly. It was said he received as loud an ovation as Jimi Hendrix.

WOODSTOCK WASN'T MEANT TO BE A FREE CONCERT.

Mounting Woodstock was not intended to be an altruistic venture. Kornfeld, Rosenman, Roberts, and Lang paid for talent, production costs, Yasgur's site, and incurred other expenses in the hope of profiting from ticket sales. One day's admission was $7; attending all three (which stretched into early Monday morning due to rain and technical delays) was $18. But as people began to show up to Bethel days before the scheduled start, the infrastructure was still incomplete. Fences still needed to be erected and ticket booths set up. With no practical way of turning away crowds, the partners decided to make it a free event for people who had not purchased one of the 100,000 tickets that had been pre-sold. Of the 400,000 who ultimately attended, 300,000 were never charged an admission fee.

MANY COWS WERE IN ATTENDANCE.

Yasgur's farm was a functioning site of business, which meant that the incoming crowds were going to be displacing the cattle usually present on site. His workers tried to corral them into a fenced area, but so many people ran over the barrier and set up campgrounds that they decided to just let the cows wander and mingle with attendees. One of Yasgur's employees, George Peavey, told United Press International that the cows and music fans "seem to be getting along together fine."

JIMI HENDRIX GOT $18,000 TO PERFORM.

Booking big-name acts didn't come cheap. Jimi Hendrix was Woodstock's highest-paid performer, earning $18,000 (roughly $125,000 in 2019 dollars, accounting for inflation). Creedence Clearwater

Revival, the first act booked, received $10,000. The Who received $6250 (although another report had them receiving $11,200) and Joe Cocker made a relatively paltry $1375. Sha Na Na got $750, while Quill got the most economic booking at $375.

ROCK N' ROLL

ROCK N' ROLL

1. What British rock band pioneered the use of the light show?
   a. Pink Floyd
   b. Led Zeppelin
   c. the Beatles
   d. the Who

2. What was the world's first "rock opera"?
   a. Spartacus
   b. Hair
   c. The Phantom of the Opera
   d. Tommy

3. What was the first rock song to become famous around the world?
   a. Hound Dog
   b. Teen Angel

c. Rock Around the Clock

d. Words of Love

4. What is the fundamental rhythmic characteristic of rock 'n' roll?
   a. the dead beat
   b. the easy beat
   c. the slow beat
   d. the back beat

5. Who was the first rock-and-roll superstar?
   a. George Harrison
   b. Madonna
   c. Elvis Presley
   d. Clyde McPhatter

6. The famous British rock group Led Zeppelin was initially known as:
   a. The Black Album
   b. The New Yardbirds
   c. Hollywood Rose
   d. Acca Dacca

7. In which year did Psychedelic rock emerge?
   a. 1975
   b. 1950
   c. 1970
   d. 1966

8. The quintessential college rock band of the 1980s, named after a dream-state condition is:
   a. Alice In Chains
   b. ZZ Top
   c. R.E.M.
   d. The Cure

9. What is the original name of American rock musician Alice Cooper?
   a. Vincent Damon Furnier
   b. Steven Tallarico

c. Gordon Sumner

d. Eric Patrick Clapton

10. Which rock band was formed in 1985 by Rose and Stradlin?

    a. Aerosmith

    b. Guns N' Roses

    c. The Eagles

    d. Nirvana

11. Name the heavy metal band that was formed by guitarist James Hetfield and drummer Lars Ulrich in 1981.

    a. Linkin Park

    b. Metallica

    c. Slipknot

    d. Led Zeppelin

12. The song "Born in the U.S.A." (1984) is associated with which singer?

    a. Clarence Clemons

    b. Billy Joel

    c. Bruce Springsteen

    d. Steven Van Zandt

13. Which rock band was designated by the Guinness Book of Records as the world's loudest band in 1972?
    a. Creedence Clearwater Revival
    b. Fleetwood Mac
    c. Deep Purple
    d. Lynyrd Skynyrd

14. Who was the self-proclaimed architect of rock and roll?
    a. Mick Jagger
    b. Little Richard
    c. David Brown
    d. Fats Domino

15. Who replaced Ozzy Osborne as Black Sabbath's lead singer?
    a. Steven Tyler
    b. Pete Townshend
    c. Jon Bon Jovi
    d. Ronnie James Dio

ANSWER KEY

ROCK N' ROLL

1. A

2. D

3. C

4. A

5. C

6. B

7. D

8. C

9. A

10. B

11. B

12. C

13. C

14. B

15. D

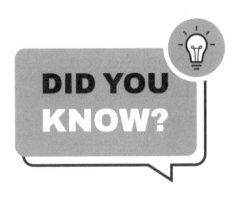

If at First You Don't Succeed

A talent manager named Jim Denny told Elvis to "stick to driving a truck because you'll never make it as a singer" after a catastrophic performance at the Grand Ole Opry. Despite this criticism, the King kept going and made rock n' roll history.

Upstaged

Little Richard kicked Jimi Hendrix out of his band in the 50's. Apparently, Hendrix refused to wear the band uniform and would steal the audience's attention with his eccentric style and guitar skills.

Homewrecker

Eric Clapton wrote the song "Layla" with the intention of stealing George Harrison's wife.

Time Is Money

Jimi Hendrix created the song "Little Wing" in a mere 145 seconds. There's being in the zone and then there's having superpowers.

Pick Up A Book

The Doors got their band name from the Aldous Huxley book, "The Doors of Perception".

Pack-A-Day

Axl Rose smoked cigarettes during a science experiment at UCLA for $8 an hour.

Say Cheese

Originally wanting to be a professional photographer, Chuck Berry started performing music so he could afford photography equipment.

Nice And Simple

ABBA got its name by taking the first letter of each band member's name.

Talent Runs In The Family

Chip Taylor wrote the song "Wild Thing," which was later performed by Hendrix. Chip is Angelina Jolie's uncle.

Schoolhouse Rock

Lynyrd Skynyrd got its name from a high school teacher, Leonard Skinner. The teacher was notorious for suspending students for having long hair. Not only did they keep their long hair, but they also came up with one of the longest guitar solos. Take that.

Cup Size

AC/DC guitarist Malcolm Young once worked as a sewing-machine mechanic in a bra factory. He must have been a master at unhooking!

Must Be This Tall To Ride

Led Zeppelin guitarist and founder, Jimmy Page, dated a 14-year-old while on tour with the band.

GUESS THE 70'S

HIT SONGS

GUESS THE 70'S HIT SONGS

1. "Once I had a love and it was a gas…"
   a. Go Away Little Girl
   b. Heart of Glass
   c. I Think I Love You

2. "I've been walkin' these streets so long…"
   a. Rhinestone Cowboy
   b. Convoy
   c. The Hustle

3. "Busted flat in Baton Rouge, waitin' for a train…"
   a. I Am Woman
   b. Want Ads
   c. Me and Bobby McGee

4. "Stuck inside these four walls, sent inside forever…"
   a. Love You Inside Out
   b. Still
   c. Band on the Run

5. "I know your eyes in the morning sun..."
   a. Making Plans For Nigel
   b. One Way Or Another
   c. How Deep Is Your Love

6. "If you need me, call me, no matter where you are..."
   a. Ain't No Mountain High Enough
   b. I'll Take You There
   c. Superstition

7. "Ooh, my little pretty one, my pretty one ..."
   a. My Sharona
   b. Mandy
   c. Best of My Love

8. "You know, I was wondering, you know..."
   a. My Sharona
   b. Don't Stop 'Til You Get Enough
   c. Stayin' Alive

9. "For so long, you and me been finding each other for so long..."
   a. Le Freak

b. Shadow Dancing
c. I Just Want to Be Your Everything

10. "My child arrived just the other day…"
    a. You're No Good
    b. Angie Baby
    c. Cat's in the Cradle

11. "Ooh, it's so good, it's so good…"
    a. I Feel Love
    b. The Night Chicago Died
    c. Whatever Gets You Thru The Night

12. "Mother, mother, there's too many of you crying…"
    a. What's Goin' On
    b. Get Down Tonight
    c. Saturday Night

13. "Holly came from Miami, F.L.A…."
    a. Southern Nights
    b. Walk On The Wild Side
    c. Boogie Fever

14. "We could hide away in daylight…"
    a. Black Water
    b. Heroes
    c. Fire

15. "We all came out to Montreux, on the Lake Geneva shoreline…"
    a. Smoke On The Water
    b. Angie
    c. Delta Dawn

16. "I ain't got no money…"
    a. I Wanna Be Your Lover
    b. My Sweet Lord
    c. September Girls

17. "Living easy, living free…"
    a. Highway to Hell
    b. Hot Child in the City
    c. Night Fever

18. "I've been really tryin', baby…"
    a. Miss You
    b. Rapper's Delight
    c. Let's Get It On

19. "In the day we sweat it out on the streets of a runaway American dream…"
    a. Rock Your Baby
    b. Born to Run
    c. My Hometown

20. "Sittin' here, eatin' my heart out waitin'…"
    a. Hot Stuff
    b. Burning
    c. You're So Vain

ANSWER KEY

GUESS THE 70'S HIT SONGS

1. B
2. A
3. C
4. C
5. C
6. A
7. A
8. B
9. C
10. C

11. A
12. A
13. B
14. B
15. A
16. A
17. A
18. C
19. B
20. A

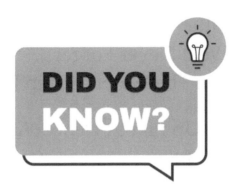

20 Songs from 70s You'll Never Forget The Lyrics

1. "It's Only Teenage Wasteland!"
    Baba O' Riley – The Who (1971)

2. "Dream Until Your Dreams Come True!"
    Dream On – Aerosmith (1973)

3. "I'm Gonna Find Ya...I'm Gonna Getcha
    Getcha Getcha Getcha!"
    One Way Or Another – Blondie (1979)

4. "From The Kentucky Coal Mine To The
    California Sun..."
    Me And Bobby McGee – Janis Joplin (1971)

5. "Season Ticket On A One Way Ride!"
    Highway To Hell – AC/DC (1979)

6. "No Matter What We Get Out Of This, I Know We'll Never Forget..."
Smoke On The Water – Deep Purple (1972)

7. "Revved Up Like A Deuce, Another Runner In The Night"
Blinded By The Light – Manfred Mann's Earth Band (1973)

8. "I'll Be Your Friend, I'll Help You Carry On..."
Lean On Me – Bill Withers (1972)

9. "If I Leave Here Tomorrow, Would You Still Remember Me?"
Free Bird – Lynyrd Skynyrd (1973)

10. "I Wanna Rock And Roll All Night And Party Every Day!"
Rock And Roll All Nite – KISS (1975)

11. "I'd Love You To Love Me, I'm Beggin' You To Beg Me."
I Want You To Want Me – Cheap Trick (1979)

12. "I Want To Live, I Want To Give. I've Been A Miner For A Heart Of Gold."
Heart Of Gold – Neil Young (1971)

13. "I Bet You Think This Song Is About You"
   You're So Vain – Carly Simon (1972)

14. "Oh Mirror In The Sky What Is Love?"
   Fleetwood Mac – Landslide (1975)

15. "Mama...Just Killed A Man."
   Bohemian Rhapsody – Queen (1975)

16. Stairway To Heaven – Led Zeppelin (1971)
   "Your Stairway Lies On The Whispering Wind..."

17. "Sweet Dreams And Flying Machines In Pieces On The Ground"
   Fire And Rain – James Taylor (1970)

18. "Such A Lovely Place... Such A Lovely Face"
   Hotel California – The Eagles (1976)

19. "You May Say I'm A Dreamer But I'm Not The Only One..."
   Imagine- John Lennon (1971)

20. "Whisper Words Of Wisdom"
   Let It Be – The Beatles (1970)

MARILYN MONROE

MARILYN MONROE

1. What was Marilyn Monroe's name at the time of her birth?
   a. Norma Jeane Mortensen
   b. Marlene Dietrich
   c. Jane Seymour
   d. Jill Dando

2. What was Marilyn Monroe's name at the time of her baptism?
   a. Norma Jeane Baker
   b. Elizabeth Smith
   c. Jane Eyre
   d. Letitia Bonaparte

3. What was Marilyn Monroe's character in Niagara?
   a. Mary Fokker
   b. Lois Lane
   c. Rose Loomis
   d. Lucy Longfellow

4. Who were Marilyn Monroe's co-stars in How to Marry a Millionaire?
   a. Clark Gable, Vivien Leigh
   b. Lauren Bacall, Betty Grable
   c. Richard Burton, Elizabeth Taylor
   d. Robert Redford, Demi Moore

5. For which film did Marilyn Monroe get the Golden Globe Award for Best Actress in a Comedy?
   a. The Prince and the Showgirl
   b. Gentlemen Prefer Blondes
   c. Bus Stop
   d. Some Like it Hot

6. In which film did Marilyn Monroe play the character of Claudia Caswell?
   a. All About Eve
   b. Ladies of the Cross
   c. The Fireball
   d. Love Nest

7. Who was Marilyn Monroe's husband from 29 June 1956 to 20 January1961?
   a. Jimmy Dougherty
   b. Arthur Miller
   c. Joe D'Maggio
   d. Aristotle Socrates Onasis

8. Where was Marilyn Monroe born?
   a. New York
   b. Philadelphia
   c. Los Angeles
   d. Austin

9. On 29 May 1962 Marilyn Monroe sang "Happy Birthday to You Mr. President". Who was the President?
   a. Dwight Eisenhower
   b. Richard Nixon

c. John Kennedy
d. Gerald Ford

10. When did Marilyn Monroe die?
    a. 19 June 1968
    b. 11 January 1964
    c. 30 November 1970
    d. 5 August 1962

ANSWER KEY

MARILYN MONROE

1. A

2. A

3. C

4. B

5. D

6. A

7. B

8. C

9. C

10. D

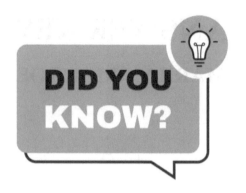

How the stage name Marilyn Monroe was created.

The stage name, Marilyn Monroe, was created with the help of Ben Lyon, the head of new talent at Fox Studios. The name Marilyn was chosen because he said to her, "You are to me a Marilyn," which was based off a woman, Marilyn Miller, he knew who starred in musicals in New York. She then asked if she could use her grandmother's last name, Monroe. And that is how Marilyn Monroe came into being.

She was sent to an orphanage when she was nine years old.

The reason she was sent to an orphanage was because her mother was hospitalized for mental issues. The issues were so debilitating for her mother that it caused her mother to spend most of the rest of her life inside some kind of mental institution.

She attempted suicide for the first time (known first attempt) after Johnny Hyde died in December 1950.

Johnny Hyde was a super agent who she was seeing romantically and who was also her agent. She credited him throughout her life with building her career and jumpstarting her path to fame.

Tony Curtis's famous line, "It was like kissing Hitler," was spoken because of how difficult it was working with Marilyn on Some Like It Hot.

She would want to do twenty to thirty takes of the same scene, and it often caused her co-stars performance to suffer as a result.

NAME THE MOVIE

USING THEME SONG

NAME THE MOVIE USING THEME SONG

1. "Five passengers set sail that day, for a three-hour tour."
   a. "Gilligan's Island"
   b. "Mr. Ed"
   c. "Rawhide"
   d. "Car 54, Where Are You?"

2. "A horse is a horse, of course, of course/And no one can talk to a horse of course."
   a. "Mr. Ed"
   b. "Flipper"
   c. "Scooby Doo, Where Are You?"
   d. "Gidget"

3. "He will sleep til noon but before it's dark/He'll have every picnic basket in Jellystone Park."
   a. "The Jetsons"
   b. "Batman"
   c. "Scooby Doo, Where Are You?"
   d. "Yogi Bear"

4. "Everyone loves the king of the sea/Ever so kind and gentle is he."
   a. "Howdy Doody"
   b. "Flipper"
   c. "Romper Room"
   d. "Thunderbirds"

5. "Here's the story of a lovely lady, who was bringing up three very lovely girls"
   a. "The Brady Bunch"
   b. "Leave It to Beaver"
   c. "That Girl"
   d. "The Patty Duke Show"

6. "Come ride the little train that is rolling down the tracks to the junction."
   a. "Captain Kangaroo"
   b. "Hogan's Heroes"
   c. "Petticoat Junction"
   d. "Bonanza"

7. "Say kids, what time is it?"
   a. "Howdy Doody"
   b. "Mr. Ed"
   c. "Scooby Doo, Where Are You?"
   d. "Huckleberry Hound"

8. "His boy Elroy/Daughter Judy/Jane -- his wife."
   a. "Flipper"
   b. "Bewitched"
   c. "Daniel Boone"
   d. "The Jetsons"

9. "They're creepy and they're kooky, mysterious and spooky."
   a. "The Addams Family"
   b. "The Brady Bunch"
   c. "Leave It to Beaver"
   d. "The Munsters"

10. "With an eye like an eagle and as tall as a mountain was he."
    a. "Daniel Boone"
    b. "The Munsters"
    c. "Gomer Pyle, U.S.M.C."
    d. "The Fugitive"

11. "I'm so glad we had this time together/Just to have a laugh or sing a song."
    a. "Father Knows Best"
    b. "Bewitched"

   c. "Howdy Doody"

   d. "The Carol Burnett Show"

12. "Come and watch us sing and play/We're the young generation/And we've got something to say."

   a. "Gidget"

   b. "The Patty Duke Show"

   c. "Flipper"

   d. "The Monkees"

13. "Rollin' rollin' rollin', keep movin' movin' movin'"

   a. "Bonanza"

   b. "The Rifleman"

   c. "Rawhide"

   d. "Car 54, Where Are You?"

14. "The end of the Civil War was near, when quite accidentally/A hero who sneezed abruptly seized retreat and reversed it to victory."

   a. "Gunsmoke"

   b. "Laramie"

c. "The Big Valley"
d. "F Troop"

15. "The most effectual/Who's intellectual."
    a. "Yogi Bear"
    b. "Top Cat"
    c. "Huckleberry Hound"
    d. "Scooby Doo, Where Are You? "

ANSWER KEY

NAME THE MOVIE USING THEME SONG

1. A

2. A

3. D

4. B

5. A

6. C

7. A

8. D

9. A

10. A

11. D

12. D

13. C

14. D

15. B

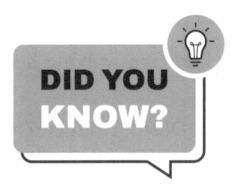

THE MOST ICONIC '60S MOVIE QUOTES

THE GRADUATE

"Mrs. Robinson, you're trying to seduce me...aren't you?" (The Graduate, 1967)

Twenty-one-year-old Benjamin Braddock (Dustin Hoffman) was way out of his league when Mrs. Robinson (Anne Bancroft) set her eyes on him. This iconic line was uttered when Mrs. Robinson sat Benjamin down and asked him what he thought of her. Since he knew her all of his life he surely had an opinion about her. As Benjamin tried to retreat, she told him to sit back down since her husband wasn't going to be home for a couple of hours. That's when he got flustered and nervously said, "Mrs. Robinson, you're trying to seduce me...aren't you?"

MIDNIGHT COWBOY

"I'm walking here! I'm walking here!" (Midnight Cowboy, 1969)

As Ratso Rizzo (Dustin Hoffman) limped down a street in New York City, he got absorbed in his conversation with Joe Buck (Jon Voight) and didn't check both ways before crossing the street. That's when a cabbie turned into the crosswalk and almost hit the pair. Rizzo slammed his hands on the hood and shouted, "I'm walking here! I'm walking here!" The line got immortalized in film history, but there was contention on its origins. Dustin Hoffman said he improvised the line, but the director, John Schlesinger, believed it was in the script.

DR. NO

"Bond. James Bond" (Dr. No, 1962)

This line is one of the most iconic quotes from the James Bond franchise, and the first time it was uttered was in Dr. No. Sean Connery muttered his character's name during the very first scene in the movie, while he was sitting at a casino table playing Baccarat.

When his opponent, Sylvia Trench, admired his lucky streak, she asked his name. The secret spy introduced himself as, "Bond. James Bond." The line became iconic.

GREATEST MOVIES

OF ALL TIME

GREATEST MOVIES OF ALL TIME

1. Who played Bob Woodward in All the President's Men?
   - a. Robert Redford
   - b. Dustin Hoffman
   - c. Jason Robards
   - d. Hal Holbrook

2. Which of the following disaster films was not released during the 1970's?
   - a. Earthquake
   - b. The Poseidon Adventure
   - c. Twister
   - d. The Towering Inferno

3. In what horror movie did Ellen Burstyn play the mother of Linda Blair?
   a. The Omen
   b. Halloween
   c. The Exorcist
   d. The Devil in Miss Jones

4. Who were the romantic characters in The Way We Were?
   a. Katie and Roger
   b. Rachel and Hubbell
   c. Rachel and Roger
   d. Katie and Hubbell

5. With what animal's blood do Carrie's tormentors douse her at the prom?
   a. Pig
   b. Goat
   c. Lamb
   d. Cow

6. Midnight Express was based on the real-life story of Billy Hayes, a college student who served time in (and later escaped from) a prison in what country?

a. Russia

b. Turkey

c. Mexico

d. Greece

7. What Burt Reynolds film included a Basset Hound character named Fred?

a. The Longest Yard

b. Deliverance

c. Smoky and the Bandit

d. Starting Over

8. What hairstyle did Bo Derek make famous in the movie "10?"

a. French Braid

b. Side ponytail

c. Cornrows

d. Pixie cut

9. In what movie did Gene Wilder (not Hackman!) implore Teri Garr to "Put. Zee Candle. BACK!"

a. Stir Crazy

b. Young Frankenstein

c. Silver Streak

d. Blazing Saddles

10. In "Heaven Can Wait," Warren Beatty plays a football player who returns to life in the body of _____?
    a. A prisoner
    b. A teacher
    c. An actor
    d. A millionaire

11. Who played Janet in The Rocky Horror Picture Show?
    a. Susan Sarandon
    b. Michelle Pfeiffer
    c. Meryl Streep
    d. Sally Field

12. In The Omen, where does Damien's father discover the "Three Sixes" birthmark?
    a. Between his toes
    b. His neck
    c. His scalp
    d. His earlobe

13. What was Dirty Harry's last name?
    a. Cunningham
    b. Johnson
    c. Smith
    d. Callahan

14. What happens on Freaky Friday?
    a. A dog and his owner switch bodies
    b. A father and son switch bodies

c. A mother and daughter switch bodies

d. A cat and a bird switch bodies

15. What animal was the focus of the movies "Willard" and "Ben?"

a. Mouse

b. Rat

c. Rabbit

d. Raccoon

16. Who was "The Jerk?"

a. Steve Martin

b. Gene Wilder

c. Richard Pryor

d. Mel Brooks

17. Where did Adrian work when she and Rocky met?

a. Skating rink

b. Grocery store

c. Bar

d. Pet store

18. In "Love Story," Jenny tells Oliver that love means never having to say _____?

a. Goodbye
b. You're wrong
c. You're sorry
d. I love you

19. Which of the following characters is not killed on Halloween?
    a. Annie
    b. Judith Myers
    c. Laurie Strode
    d. Lynda

20. In what movie did a college cafeteria "Food Fight!" occur?
    a. High Anxiety
    b. Animal House
    c. Young Frankenstein
    d. 1941

21. Which of the following James Bond films was NOT made in the 1970's?
    a. Moonraker
    b. The Spy Who Loved Me
    c. Goldfinger
    d. Diamonds Are Forever

22. What film contains characters named (among others) Veruca Salt, Violet Beauregarde, Augustus Gloop, and Arthur Slugworth?
    a. Willy Wonka and the Chocolate Factory
    b. Pete's Dragon
    c. Mad Max
    d. Monty Python and the Holy Grail

23. What film is known for using Scott Joplin's "The Entertainer" as the musical score?
    a. The Great Gatsby
    b. The Godfather
    c. The Goodbye Girl
    d. The Sting

24. "It's gonna take you and the police department and the fire department and the National Guard to get me outta here!"
    a. The Outlaw Josie Wales
    b. Norma Rae
    c. Alice Doesn't Live Here Anymore
    d. Star Wars

25. What happens at the very end of Kramer vs. Kramer?
    a. The dad loses custody of his son
    b. The mom loses custody of her son
    c. The mom hands over custody of her son
    d. The dad hands over custody of his son

ANSWER KEY

GREATEST MOVIES OF ALL TIME

1. A
2. C
3. C
4. D
5. A
6. B
7. C
8. C
9. B
10. D
11. A
12. C
13. D
14. C
15. B
16. A

17. D
18. C
19. B
20. C
21. C
22. A
23. D
24. B
25. C

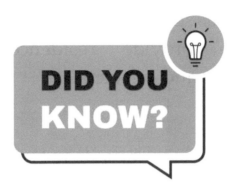

11 THINGS YOU DID NOT KNOW
ABOUT HOLYWOOD

1. The Jazz Singer is a movie made in 1927, it is the first film with sound, and it cost the astonishing amount of $422,000 to be made.

2. The famous Hollywood sign was made in 1923 and it cost $21,000.

3. Four brothers, who were trade soap salesman in Ohio, set up in Hollywood one of the first movie studios, in 1918. They called it Warner Brothers.

4. The famous Diplomat Hotel was opened in 1958, to provide residence for many entertainers and celebrities.

5. The first movie ever made in Hollywood was in 1910 and it was called In Old California. It was only 17 minutes long.

6. In 1932 the 24 year old actress Peg Entwistle, committed suicide by jumping from the letter "H" of the Hollywood sign. Today many people believe that the sign is haunted by her ghost.

7. Hugh Hefner is a huge fan of the industry and he donated $27,000 for the Hollywood sign restoration.

8. In 1976 some vandals modified the sign to "Hollyweed".

9. The first person that had his star engraved on Hollywood: Walk of Fame is Stanley Kramer.

10. In 1994, nearly 450 stars were removed from Hollywood: Walk of Fame during a subway construction.

11. Who's Afraid of Virginia Woolf is the most expensive film that was made in black and white; it cost $7.5 million.

LIGHTS, CAMERA

ACTION!

LIGHTS, CAMERA, ACTION!

1. The code in The Matrix comes from what food recipes?
    a. Sushi recipes
    b. Dumpling recipes
    c. Stir-fry recipes
    d. Pad thai recipes

2. What's the name of Meatloaf's character in The Rocky Horror Picture Show?
    a. Henry
    b. Eddie
    c. Chuck
    d. Al

3. Who actually drew the sketch of Rose in Titanic?
    a. Leonardo DiCaprio
    b. Billy Zane
    c. James Cameron
    d. Kathy Bates

4. Who voices Joy in Pixar's Inside Out?
    a. Tina Fey
    b. Kathryn Hahn
    c. Ellen DeGeneres
    d. Amy Poehler

5. Where were The Lord of the Rings movies filmed?
   a. Ireland
   b. Iceland
   c. New Zealand
   d. Australia

6. Which country does Forrest Gump travel to as part of the All-American Ping-Pong Team?
   a. Vietnam
   b. China
   c. Sweden
   d. France

7. Which famous Pulp Fiction scene was filmed backward?
   a. Vincent and Mia's dance scene
   b. Mia's overdose scene
   c. The royale with cheese scene
   d. The Ezekiel 25:17 scene

8. Which actor was in the following movies: The Outsiders, Wayne's World, and Tommy Boy?
   a. Tom Cruise
   b. Matt Dillon

    c. Rob Lowe

    d. C. Thomas Howell

9. Who was the first Black person to win an Oscar?

    a. Hattie McDaniel

    b. Sidney Poitier

    c. Dorothy Dandridge

    d. James Earl Jones

10. Freddy Krueger wears a striped sweater that is which colors?

    a. Red and blue

    b. Orange and green

    c. Red and green

    d. Orange and brown

11. Who did the cat in The Godfather belong to?

    a. Francis Ford Coppola

    b. Diane Keaton

    c. Al Pachino

    d. No one — the cat was a stray

12. Which movie is this famous line from: "I wish I knew how to quit you."

    a. Love Actually

b. How to Lose a Guy in 10 Days

c. Brokeback Mountain

d. The Notebook

13. Which movie is this quote from: "Here's looking at you, kid."
    a. Breakfast at Tiffany's
    b. Citizen Kane
    c. Casablanca
    d. Notorious

14. What is the name of the camp where counselors are terrorized by a slasher in Friday the 13th?
    a. Camp Holland Lake
    b. Camp Crystal Lake
    c. Camp Diamond Lake
    d. Camp Green Lake

15. What object was Toy Story's Woody originally?
    a. A ventriloquist dummy
    b. A puppet
    c. A clown doll
    d. A nesting doll

ANSWER KEY

LIGHTS, CAMERA, ACTION!

1. A
2. B
3. C
4. D
5. C
6. B
7. B
8. C
9. A
10. C
11. D
12. C
13. C
14. B
15. A

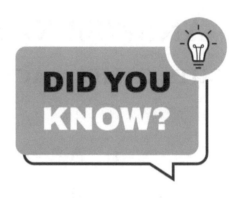

FASCINATING FACTS
ABOUT THE FILM INDUSTRY

The first toilet did not flush on the American big screen until 1960

Alfred Hitchcock's "Psycho" features the first shot of a flushing toilet in mainstream American cinema. Marion Crane, played by Janet Leigh, flushes a piece of paper, setting up the audience for the infamous "shower" scene, wherein Hitchcock kills off his leading lady midway through the movie.

The first narrative film is under 12 minutes long

Though it was not the first film ever made, the 1903 film "The Great Train Robbery" was the first film that told a story and is considered the first narrative fiction film. Under 12 minutes long, it was produced by Thomas Edison's Edison Studios. The film shoot took place in New Jersey.

The first drive-in theater opened in 1933

On June 6, 1933, Richard Hollingshead opened the first drive-in theater in Camden, New Jersey. People watched the British comedy "Wives Beware" after paying 25 cents per car. Though the drive-in's popularity has waxed and waned through the decades, 321 theaters remained open in the United States as of June 2020.

The White House has a movie theater

The first film to screen at the White House, D.W. Griffith's "The Birth of a Nation," was screened in the main building. In 1942, when the East Wing of the White House was built, President Franklin D. Roosevelt turned the East Terrace cloakroom into a movie theater. The theater features 42 seats to accommodate the First Family and their guests.

The film rating system began in 1968

Motion pictures were first rated in 1968 based on a family-focused rating system. Motion Picture

Association of America (MPAA) chairman Jack Valenti replaced the infamous Hays Code with the new guidelines.

The first motion-picture film camera was called the Kinetoscope

Invented by Thomas Edison and William D**kson, the camera allowed for one individual to view a film through a peephole window at the top of the device. The only surviving film from the Kinetoscope is the 1890 test film "Monkeyshines, No. 1."

The first curse word appeared in film in 1929

Cursing didn't show up in film until two years after sound did. In the decades that followed, swearing became common, especially in American cinema. The film that featured the most use of the F-word is Martin Scorsese's "The Wolf of Wall Street."

The first public movie theater opened after the turn of the 20th century

In Pittsburgh, Pennsylvania on June 19, 1905, the Nickelodeon theater opened. The owner, vaudeville organizer Harry Davis, opened more than a dozen Nickelodeon theaters in Pittsburgh within a few months. More than 8,000 cinemas cropped up within two years.

The first film kiss happened in 1896

A 30-second film called "The Kiss" was the first kiss captured on film. It featured Broadway stars May Irwin and John Rice kissing. The film was produced by Thomas Edison's company in 1896.

The first public movie screening was held in 1895 in Paris.

The Lumière brothers debuted the film "La sortie des ouvriers de l'usine Lumière (Workers Leaving the Lumière Factory)" at the very first public film screening on December 28, 1895. The black-and-white film was only 50 seconds long and depicted the Lumière factory as several workers were leaving.

DON'T FORGET TO LEAVE AN AMAZON REVIEW

We hope that you enjoyed playing and answering these trivia questions. Were you able to get most of the answers? *Trivia for Seniors: Music and Movies Edition* was created to entertain, challenge, and bring mental stimulation to readers while reliving great music and movies from the past while having fun.

See you at our next trivia game!

OTHER BOOKS YOU MAY LIKE
SENIOR BRAIN WORKOUTS

Aging is inevitable, but brain fitness can be something that you can always be prepared. Never think twice, aging is bound to happen no matter how you avoid it. Train your brain as early as now.

SENIOR BRAIN WORKOUT BOOK 1:
Trivia for Seniors: 365 Fun and Exciting Questions and Riddles and That Will Test Your Memory, Challenge Your Thinking, And Keep Your Brain Young

Find it on Amazon at:

http://bit.ly/TriviaforSeniors

SENIOR BRAIN WORKOUT BOOK 2:

Trivia for Seniors: Keep Your Brain Young with 365 Exciting and Challenging Questions of Events from the 50s, 60s, 70s, and 80s!

Find it on Amazon at:
https://bit.ly/TriviaforSeniorsBook2

SENIOR BRAIN WORKOUT BOOK 3:

Trivia for Seniors: Random and Funny Edition.
365 Hilariously Random Questions That Will Test Your Wit, Develop Your Sense of Humor and Keep Your Brain Young

Find it on Amazon at:
https://bit.ly/TriviaforSeniorsBook3

SENIOR BRAIN WORKOUT BOOK 4:

Trivia for Seniors: All-American Edition. 365 Fun and Stimulating Questions That Will Challenge Your Memory, Test Your American History, And Keep Your Brain Young

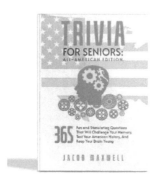

Find it on Amazon at:
https://bit.ly/TriviaforSeniorsBook4

SENIOR BRAIN WORKOUT BOOK 5:

Bible Trivia for Seniors: A Fun, Brain-Boosting Question Game to Test Your Knowledge of Scripture, Strengthen Your Faith, and Keep Your Brain Young

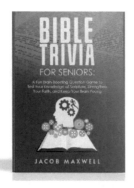

Find it on Amazon at:
https://bit.ly/TriviaforSeniorsBook5

SENIOR FITNESS

Exercise is undeniably important- even more so for seniors. Exercises and weight training into old age has been proven to be one of the keys to longevity and vitality. Many seniors feel intimated by exercising because of the risks and pain associated with it. Let me tell you that, with the right guide, just about anyone can begin an exercise routine and improve their physique! In Senior Fitness, I try to do just that- provide you with a guide that will test your level of fitness and offer you tailored workout routines and customizable exercises that will adjust to your needs.

If you're ready to get fit and feel at least 10 years younger, then get your copy of Senior Fitness today!

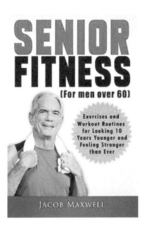

Find it on Amazon at:

http://bit.ly/SeniorFitn

Made in United States
Troutdale, OR
03/05/2024

18235939R10146